# LA CUISINE DE
# JOËL ROBUCHON

First published in 1993 by
Les Editions du Chêne–Hachette Livre as
*Les Dimanches de Joël Robuchon*

With the participation of Nicolas de Rabaudy
Photography by Hervé Amiard
Art Design by Laurence Mouton
Foreword by Alain Genestar

Copyright © Société Nouvelle des Editions du Chêne
– *Le Journal du Dimanche,* 1993

This paperback edition first published in 2001 by
Cassell Paperbacks, Cassell & Co
Wellington House, 125 Strand
London, WC2R 0BB

Distributed in the United States of America by
Sterling Publishing Co., Inc.
387 Park Avenue South,
New York, NY 10016-8810

A CIP catalogue record for this book is available
from the British Library

ISBN 1-84188-134-1

# LA CUISINE DE
# JOËL ROBUCHON

WITH
NICOLAS DE RABAUDY

PHOTOGRAPHS BY
HERVÉ AMIARD

STYLING BY
LAURENCE MOUTON

PREFACE BY
ALAIN GENESTAR

CASSELLPAPERBACKS

# .PREFACE.

## *The story of a meeting and of a book*

It was summer. All of Paris was on holiday, just as it is every year. That particular day, I dined with a few friends at Joël Robuchon's restaurant. I did not know him personally, only by hearsay. He was said to be France's greatest chef. And it was said that his cuisine was the most beautiful, marvellous and delicate in the world. Yes, I thought, but wasn't there among this avalanche of compliments and flattery a certain Parisian snobbery that comes with exaggerated fashions and is as fleeting as are all fashions? A journalist always mistrusts hearsay and often confuses it with rumour.

And then, I found myself at table that summer . . .

It was hot outside the Trocadéro and so lovely at our table. For two hours I ate the stuff of dreams, revelling in an exquisite dinner set in charming surroundings. In a rare occurrence for a dinner among journalist friends, we hardly spoke of current events or exchanged opinions on the latest happenings, either big or small. Our only commentary, which was uttered in hushed whispers as if we had been at prayer, revolved around the meal before us. Between us there was no debate – rather, there was a competition of eulogies, a rivalry over the words we could use to describe the delicate marriage of colours and fine ingredients on our plates. Words can barely describe what we sensed from the very first bite – there was silence, our eyes were half-closed – for they are inadequate to express the ecstasy of the moment as we tasted each morsel and then waited breathlessly and expectantly for the next course.

I will always remember the menu we were served that day, as Proust did his madeleine. There were new and interesting associations, from caviar to cauliflower, a Colbert whiting which was followed by a young lamb of an unrivalled spring-like tenderness, accompanied by a pure and divine purée, and many more delights, all of them marvellous, culminating in unforgettable yet simple desserts, such as Robuchon's chocolate tart. The hearsay had been correct.

And then there was a meeting...

Joël Robuchon joined us in the salon at the end of our meal. The master of the starred restaurants, the star himself (a cliché which does not suit him at all) a simple man. He is not shy, but is soft-spoken and humble, respectful of his art and he was anxious to know our impressions. He waited for a remark, smiling expectantly. Then he explained how he never tires of working, researching and continually trying to improve his efforts. I took him aside and explained that, starting in autumn, the *Journal du Dimanche* was going to gather together the best chroniclers, including the renowned Françoise Giroud, one of France's best food writers, to talk about books each week. And I invited him to join us.

Joel consented. He agreed, first of all, both to create a beautiful project and to contribute a 'first' to the paper: he would pen a real culinary chronicle, which would not only present a recipe, but would also recount a bit of history and passion … a 'saga' of the featured ingredient, whether young hare or oysters, guinea fowl or lobsters, caviar or potatoes, that formed the genesis of his inimitable cuisine. These are like the notes which the composer places on his score. They are like the words which, strung together, make a book. These are the everyday characters you will find parading on generic menus. As a reviewer writes about books, Joël

Robuchon agreed to write about his art, recounting the lives of his characters, describing and elucidating their mysteries, sometimes scorning their shortcomings and, at others, blessing their unions or couplings with various ingredients, both exceptional and ordinary. His is a living art. Robuchon makes his ingredients live, breathe, and sing. He leads the reader through his stories, until the denouement, when the intrigue rushes to a final climax: the recipe itself. True to his word, Joël Robuchon has created a culinary and literary adventure.

And then, the book was born …

Each Wednesday evening, before going to press for a Sunday publication, I read Robuchon's passionate and minutely detailed text, which drew on his extensive knowledge and personal reading. There were 52 moments of happiness in all, which today comprise a beautiful cookbook and history, written by my friend, the great author of French cuisine.

Alain Genestar
Editorial Director
*Journal du Dimanche*

# A BRIEF GLOSSARY OF TERMS

| | |
|---|---|
| Aubergine...........................................Eggplant | Greaseproof paper.....................................Waxed paper |
| Caster sugar.........................Superfine sugar | Grill...................................................................Broiler |
| Clingfilm....................................Plastic wrap | Icing sugar....................................Confectioner's sugar |
| Courgette......................................Zucchini | Offal..............................................................Innards |
| Double cream...........................Heavy cream | Single cream.......................Half-and-half or light cream |

# .TABLE OF CONTENTS.

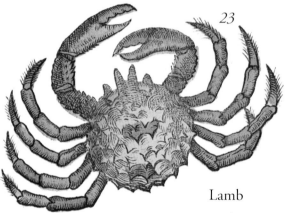

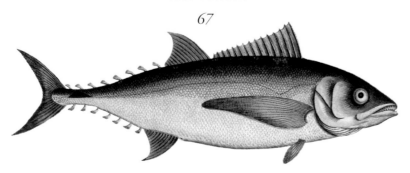

# AUTUMN

## WINTER

SPRING

# .ASPARAGUS.

Incomparable and always seductive, the delicate asparagus makes its appearance in March. Once regarded as an aphrodisiac, it was banned from the tables of 19th-century nunneries. Though many varieties of asparagus exist, the most coveted are those grown in Lauris – in the South of France – which are prized for their distinctive flavour. Purple asparagus from Argenteuil, where hybridization has yielded many other strains of this vegetable, possesses a varying degree of bitterness. White asparagus, which is cultivated on the plains, has a more subtle flavour. The marvellous wild asparagus is the rarest gem of all.

*Everyone loves asparagus, that most seductive of vegetables.*

To appreciate asparagus, freshness must be given first priority, since it is the best guarantee of tenderness. Check the stalks to be sure that they are rigid and smooth, without too many scales, and that the tips are firmly attached. The stalks should be fresh and have a healthy lustre; the ends should be in good condition and they should feel heavy in your hand. You should be able to press a fingernail gently through the outer skin of the edible part. The real test is to snap off the end of a stalk and check that the break is clean and the stalk is not dry. To obtain a uniform cooking, I recommend choosing asparagus of the same diameter.

Asparagus must be eaten as soon as possible, preferably the same day it is picked, since it does not store well. If it is absolutely necessary to store it, do so for no more than two or three days. Wrap it in a moist cloth so that it has the least possible contact with air and light, and keep it in the vegetable drawer of the refrigerator.

To prepare asparagus, remove the scales with a paring knife, starting just below the head of the spear, all the way down to the base of the stalk. This will uncover dirt and sand that neither washing nor cooking will eliminate. Scrape the stalk with a potato peeler from the tip toward the base, peeling as carefully as possible in order to preserve the essential shape of the asparagus, as much for aesthetic reasons as for uniformity of cooking. Place the spears in a basin of cold water, wash well, and drain. Group them according to their diameter, since the cooking time varies according to thickness, size and weight. Once sorted, gently tie the bunches with two loops of thread, one about 2 inches (5 cm) from the head, the other 3 inches (7.5 cm) further down. The tops of the stalks should be aligned, and the bases should be cut so that they are even; the total length of the asparagus should be 7 inches (18 cm) at most.

Asparagus may be steamed, but doing so diminishes its colour – a pity, especially if you are using the pretty, vivid green variety. It is better to cook it in simmering salted water. The best method is to stand the spears, tops up, in a tall, narrow saucepan for several minutes, so that they cook faster. Then gently press the ends of the spears, which should be pliable enough to allow the whole stalk to immerse. Since asparagus floats, keep a clean cloth handy to cover the pot; this holds in the steam and keeps the cooking uniform. It is important not to overcook asparagus. Test it by gently piercing the top of a spear with the point of a knife. There should be a slight resistance, but the asparagus should not be crisp. Once it is done, take the bunches out of the pot, taking care not to break the stalks, and let them drain. Place the asparagus on a platter and serve warm.

There are some restaurateurs who cook asparagus in advance and reheat it as the orders come in, but this is a method I find repugnant. Asparagus loses its delicacy if saturated in water. If for some reason you find that there will be a delay before it is served, take it out of the pot and plunge it into ice-cold water for 10 seconds, drain it, wrap it in a damp cloth and keep it warm. When you are ready to serve it, put it back into the original cooking water and reheat it without allowing the water to boil. Traditionally, asparagus is served with vinaigrette, mayonnaise or, more elegantly, covered with Chantilly mayonnaise, hollandaise sauce, mousseline sauce or maltaise sauce.

If you have a penchant for asparagus with eggs, try it in an omelette or with scrambled or soft-boiled eggs. With any of these, green asparagus is best; its white counterpart lends itself better to more classical meals. Asparagus may be served with either meat or fish; it goes well with offal and sweetbreads. The tips make excellent trimmings for any number of salads and hors-d'oeuvres.

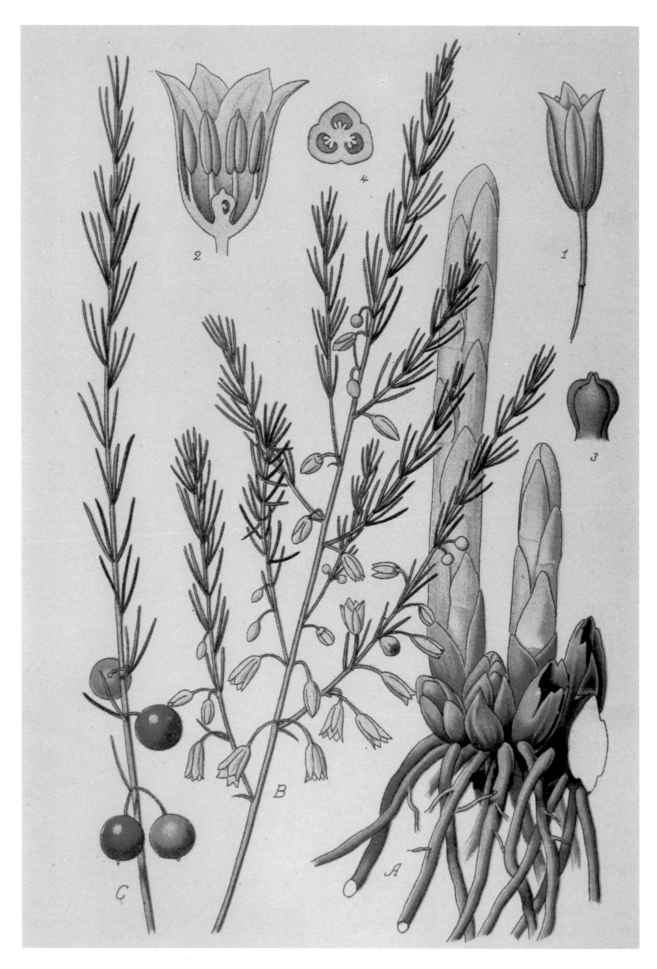

# ASPARAGUS WITH MOUSSELINE SAUCE

SERVES: 4

4 1/2 lb (2 kg) large
asparagus
9 oz (250g) butter
4 egg yolks
2 tablespoons water
2 tablespoons crème fraîche
1/2 lemon
salt, cayenne pepper

1. Prepare and cook the asparagus as indicated on page 12, preparing the sauce in the meantime.

2. Clarify the butter by melting it in a bain-marie and straining off the clear liquid that remains when the milky residue has fallen to the bottom of the pan.

3. Put the clarified butter aside, keeping it warm.

4. In a saucepan, combine the egg yolks and the water. Do not add salt. Blend them with a whisk and place the saucepan in a bain-marie. Heat the water in the bain-marie until it is simmering gently. Briskly whisk the eggs. The mixture should froth right from the start.

5. The mixture will thicken and become creamy, increasing its volume by half. When stirring in an S-shaped motion, you should be able to see the bottom of the pan. At this point, take the saucepan out of the bain-marie.

6. Add salt and pepper to the eggs. Place a tea towel underneath the pan to stabilize it. With a small ladle, add the butter little by little and whisk the mixture briskly, as you would a mayonnaise. Do not add the milky residue which has fallen to the bottom of the pan.

7. Continue stirring until the clarified butter has been completely blended in.

8. For a smoother sauce, run the mixture through a conical strainer. Your hollandaise is ready. You may add a squeeze of lemon if you wish.

9. To make the mousseline, add the *crème fraîche* (kept at room temperature) at the last minute. Check the seasoning, and keep the mousseline warm.

10. Put the mousseline in a sauce boat and arrange the warm asparagus on a napkin placed on a platter.

*This recipe is best accompanied by a Château Châlon for its aromatic complexity and smoothness.*

# .ARTICHOKES.

The artichoke is indeed only a thistle, but it is also a gourmet vegetable. With its finely carved leaves and its fragrant rounded velvety blue flower, it is the kitchen garden's crowning glory. The spear-shaped petals, discreetly armed with little claws, give an impression of extreme toughness. Nonetheless, the artichoke is a tender vegetable.

*It is only a thistle, but how tender it is!*

Artichokes are harvested from the beginning of April to the end of November, and the season commences with the small variety from the South of France. Then come the plump, flat-nosed artichokes of Brittany. In July, the excellent Macau variety from the Bordeaux region give way to the purple Rhône Valley variety.

A good artichoke should be freshly cut, which you can detect by looking at the stalk. It should be heavy in your hand and of a pure colour, without dark spots, and with tightly packed brittle leaves. When preparing an artichoke, never cut off the stem – it is best to break it off, which will remove as much fibrous material as possible from the base. To do this, hold the artichoke on the edge of the table. Take the stem in your other hand and break it at the base of the artichoke by bending it.

Artichokes may be enjoyed any number of ways. The youngest (in particular the smaller varieties) may be eaten raw with a pinch of salt and a little butter. The bigger ones are usually cooked *à l'anglaise*, in a full pot of boiling salted water. The artichokes are done when the large leaves at the base may be removed without difficulty. Refresh them, cut off the tops of the leaves, then remove the finer leaves in the centre along with the choke. Serve with a vinaigrette.

It is not generally known, except among professional cooks, how to trim raw artichokes. It is best not to remove the leaves after cooking, since doing it then strips much of the flesh as well. Once the stem has been broken off, arm yourself with a knife (preferably a stainless steel one) and detach the base of the artichoke by peeling the leaves that surround it, rather like peeling an orange. Continue until you are about 1 1/2 inches (3 cm) above the base, then cut the top third of the rest of the leaves. Pull out the central leaves until the choke is exposed. With a large spoon, loosen the choke and scrape it out thoroughly. The choke may be removed after cooking, but I suggest doing this beforehand, even if it is more difficult, as the hearts of the artichokes will be much whiter. Throughout this delicate operation, regularly rub the bottom of the artichoke with half a lemon; without this precaution, the tannic acid in the vegetable will stain your hands and darken the flesh. As soon as the choke has been removed, squeeze generous amounts of lemon juice over the heart. Place the artichoke in a basin filled with cold water that has been seasoned with lemon juice, and leave it there until all the artichokes are ready for cooking.

In a large pot, bring water to the boil. Add salt (approximately 1/2 oz/15 g of salt per 1 3/4 pt/1 litre) and the juice of a whole lemon. Add 5 tablespoons of olive oil. I do not recommend the traditional practice of adding flour to the water to preserve the colour of the hearts – the lemon juice and olive oil do the job quite nicely. Add the artichoke hearts and simmer for 15 to 20 minutes. If there are a large number, cover the pot with a cloth so that the cooking will be uniform. When they are done, remove the artichoke hearts with a slotted spoon.

Artichokes may be kept in the refrigerator for 2 or 3 days before they are eaten, as long as they are stored in the juices in which they were cooked. The hearts may be served warm, whole or quartered, seasoned with a vinaigrette or mixed in a salad. Alternatively, they may be served hot, stuffed with mushrooms or with a dressing of cheese soufflé, or, with a bit of ingenuity, used with leftovers. Sautéed or braised in butter, they make a fine garnish for fish and meat. They are excellent puréed. The hearts may also be thinly sliced in a salad, but if they are eaten raw, they should always be sprinkled liberally with lemon juice to avoid discoloration.

Turpin P.

Lambert F. sculp

# ARTICHOKE HEARTS
# AND CHICKEN LIVER SALAD

**For this delicate appetizer,
fried foie gras
may be substituted
for chicken livers.**
SERVES 2
**3 large artichokes
2 lemons
2 chicken livers
(or 2 little rounds
of raw foie gras)
salt and pepper
butter
red wine vinegar, olive oil
7 oz (200 g) mâche, washed
chervil, chives**

1. Prepare the artichoke hearts as indicated on page 16. Once they are cooked, remove with a slotted spoon and place them on a plate.

2. Separate the two lobes of each chicken liver and remove any remaining traces of bile. Add salt and pepper. In a frying pan, melt a knob of butter and rapidly brown the liver. Remove the liver from the pan and set aside, reserving the juice in the pan.

3. Slice the warm artichoke hearts and put them in a bowl. Prepare a vinaigrette, combining a large tablespoon of wine vinegar, a pinch of salt and 3 tablespoons of olive oil. Add pepper. Mix well and pour a spoonful onto the *mâche.* Toss the salad and pour the rest of the vinaigrette over the artichoke hearts. Gently stir.

4. Arrange the *mâche* decoratively on the plates, then top with the artichokes.

5. Slice the chicken livers and arrange them delicately on top of the artichokes.

6. Reheat the frying pan in which the chicken livers were cooked and deglaze it with 1 teaspoon of red wine vinegar. With a wooden spatula, loosen the juices on the bottom of the pan, bring to the boil, then pour the sauce over the chicken livers. Add pepper and sprinkle the salad with a few sprigs of chervil and chopped chives.

*As for wine,
I recommend a pleasant,
fruity Brouilly.*

# .MORELS.

The morel, that herald of the spring, only appears from the end of March until May. As mythic as it is mystical, nature's precious gift grows at the edge of the forest or in the middle of fields, but often seems to prefer imaginative places, flourishing in such unexpected spots as abandoned houses, under heaps of old papers, or in waterlogged soil. One specialist in mycology even discovered them flourishing in the cracks of the famed cobblestone streets of Paris!

The morel is a mysterious hollow mushroom, distinguishable by its honeycombed conical hood that bears a striking resemblance to a sponge. There exist no fewer than 20 different species of morels, and they may be beige, black, grey, sometimes white, purple or even greenish in colour. Several different methods of cultivation have been attempted, with unreliable results. But, for all the lack of success in cultivating this mushroom, there has been some small progress in the reproduction of its powerful aroma. Indeed, recent biotechnological developments seem to indicate that we may not be far from this goal.

As is the case with many other mushrooms, morels contain haemolysins, toxic elements that are destroyed by heat. Though morels are poisonous if eaten raw, incidents of poisoning are relatively rare. Nevertheless, it is necessary to take the utmost care in preparing them.

Some amateur cooks claim that morels should not be washed. However, I find that there is no other way

*Morels*

*with asparagus:*

*the perfect*

*combination.*

to remove minuscule grains of soil and sand which, despite the most minute of examinations, remain lodged in the mushroom's gills. They require careful washing. This is the most complex part of the preparation, which should be undertaken immediately before cooking – no earlier. First, cut off the ends of the stalks, then slice the morels in half lengthwise and check them for insects and slugs. With a fine brush, gently scrub them and then rinse them one by one in running water. Never soak morels; doing so will dilute the subtle aroma which gives this delicate mushroom all its flavour. Next, dry them thoroughly with a clean cloth.

Morels should be eaten as plain as possible – simply sauté them in butter with a sprinkling of shallots which have been left to sweat in butter beforehand. Once the mushrooms have been cooked, remove them and save their juices; cream added at the end of cooking will enhance the morels' delicate aroma. Served with veal or poultry, morels confer an incomparable delicacy on the main course. True gourmets crave them in omelettes, or with scrambled eggs; it could almost be said that the morel has signed a pact with the egg, since it infuses the egg with its aroma, enhancing its flavour. Morels may also be served in their own juices. Cut them in half and sauté them briskly over a high heat, adding the juices of any roast meat. Season and baste them frequently. But personally, I think morels are best served with asparagus.

# BRAISED MORELS AND ASPARAGUS WITH CHERVIL

1. Halve the morels. Clean them with a fine brush and rinse under running water. Do not soak. Dry them carefully.

2. Cut off the stalks. Select about 4 oz (100g) of the less pretty morels and add them to the cut-off stalks; place the caps and stalks in the chicken stock, which has been brought to a boil. Cover the pot and simmer for 20 minutes over a low heat. Then run the mushrooms and the liquid through the food processor, using a fine blade. Return the mixture to the heat and allow to reduce until you have 8 fl oz (250 ml) of liquid.

3. Take the chicken stock off the heat and add the cornflour, blended with 3 tablespoons of water. Place the pan back on the heat and bring the mixture to a boil. Then add the cream. Stir, allow it to simmer, then strain. Add 2 oz (50g) of butter and emulsify. Season

---

SERVES 4

**1 1/4 lb (500g) morels**

**18 fl oz (500 ml) chicken stock**

**1/3 oz (10g) cornflour**

**3 fl oz (75 ml) single cream**

**5 oz (150g) butter**

**3 drops tabasco sauce**

**20 large stalks asparagus**

**1 chopped shallot**

**chervil, salt and pepper**

---

with a few drops of tabasco sauce.

4. Cook the asparagus in boiling salted water. Drain, then roll it in butter in a saucepan.

5. Heat the remaining butter in a frying pan, add the chopped shallots and allow them to sweat without browning. Once they are done, add the morels to the pan and sauté; sprinkle with salt and pepper.

6. Cover the bottom of a shallow bowl with the morel cream sauce. Add the morels, then arrange the asparagus spears in a circle, alternately pointing out and in. Sprinkle with a few sprigs of chervil.

*Serve with a golden white wine,*
*such as the robust and spicy*
*1979 Château d'Arlay.*

# .SPIDER CRAB.

Certainly the tastiest of all the crustaceans, the spider crab is found in abundance along the coasts of France. This primitive-looking animal, with its spiny carapace, spindly hairy legs and elongated pincers, is greatly appreciated for its fine, delicate flesh and aroma.

Its reddish shell is no wider than 10 inches (25 cm) across, whereas the giant crabs that flourish off the Japanese coasts grow to 16 inches (40 cm), and have legs that span 10 ft (3 m). In spite of its nightmarish aspect, this crab is in fact a docile creature. Its little pincers are not a formidable defence. When it feels threatened, its first reaction is to keep stock still. If it is not left in peace, it then raises its claws to protect itself, a relatively inoffensive gesture. In contrast to the many other varieties of crab, the spider crab never leaves the ocean. Its well-developed eyes identify colours and contours; its handicap is that it cannot shed its shell once it reaches maturity, which also renders it incapable of regenerating any lost limbs.

Choose your crab while it is alive; it should be full and heavy in your hand. The female has more delicate flesh, and may be identified by raising the little tongue on the underside of her shell: the male's is much thinner than the female's.

Make the most of this delicate crustacean by simply boiling it. The flesh is flavourful, the brown creamy meat very sought after. Your first step should be to wash the crab in running water then, if necessary, brush it in order to remove any impurities which might spoil its taste while it cooks. Check to be sure none of the legs are damaged. If they are, plug the orifice with a piece of bread kneaded between your fingers. Without this precaution, the crabmeat will seep out as it cooks. Cook spider crabs as soon after buying them as possible; their flavour depends on freshness.

The court-bouillon used to boil the crab should be fragrant and spicy, so that the flavours penetrate the flesh that lines the shell. In a large pot, boil 4 pt (2 1/4

*This wonderful little crab is the most flavoursome of crustaceans.*

litres) with 1 1/2 oz (40g) of coarse sea salt, 1/2 oz (15g) of whole black peppercorns, a teaspoon of coriander seeds, 4 slivers of orange peel, 3 carrots sliced crosswise, 2 onions cut in rings, 5 cloves of garlic, a branch of fresh thyme, half a bay leaf, a sprig of basil, a piece of fresh ginger, a quarter of star anise and a pinch of fennel seeds. Cover and cook for 20 minutes. Add 1 1/4 pt (750 ml) of dry white wine and 3 1/2 fl oz (100 ml) of vinegar. (If these last ingredients are added with the others at the beginning, their acidity will prevent the vegetables from cooking normally and blending their flavours.) Bring the pot back to a boil, then add the crabs. Let them simmer for 15 to 20 minutes. Take the pot off the heat and leave to cool before removing the crabs; this way, they will steep in all the seasonings. If possible, avoid putting the crabs in the refrigerator once they have been cooked, since the cold will alter their flavour. Serve as soon as possible after cooking.

Spider crabs may be served whole or shelled. To extract the meat, first break off the legs, then open them with a nutcracker and remove the meat. Open the crab body by inserting the point of a knife between the shell and the breastplate. Empty the shell completely, first by spooning out the brown creamy meat and placing it in a bowl. Then carefully remove the white meat and place it in a bowl with the meat from the claws. Using a whisk, mix the brown meat with a little mustard and salt and pepper, then add olive oil a little at a time, as you would while making a mayonnaise, to achieve a rich sauce. Finish with a splash of vinegar and put the mixture through a fine sieve. Add chopped herbs and mix the white meat with the sauce.

There are many other ways to prepare crab. Once the flesh has been removed, you may also prepare hot dishes. The following is a good example.

# AROMATIC SEA CRAB

1. Boil the crabs as described on page 22 for 15 to 20 minutes. Allow them to cool in the court-bouillon then extract the crabmeat.

2. Wash and dry the vegetables. Peel the courgette, reserving the skin. Skin and quarter the pepper. Use only the caps of the mushrooms. Finely dice all the vegetables. Squeeze lemon juice over the mushrooms to prevent them discolouring.

3. Blanch the red pepper and the courgette peel separately in boiling salted water. Refresh and drain well. Mix all the diced vegetables together.

4. Using a fork, blend about 14 oz (400g) of crabmeat with the egg whites, cream and freshly ground black pepper.

5. Grease 12 x 6 inch (15 cm) squares of aluminium foil with a little of the butter and place equal portions of the crabmeat mixture in the centre of

**SERVES 4**

**4 lb (2 kg) large**
**live spider crabs**
**1 courgette**
**1 red pepper**
**5 white mushrooms**
**1/2 lemon**
**2 egg whites**
**2 fl oz (50 ml) cream**
**salt and pepper**
**4 oz (100g) butter**
**1 sprig of saffron**
**1 pinch of thyme flowers**
**1 teaspoon curry powder**
**ground coriander**
**2 teaspoons**
**olive oil**

each. Mould them into small rolls, pinching the ends well to ensure they are watertight.

6. Cook the rolls in simmering water for about 3 minutes. Drain them then take the crab rolls out of the foil and toss them in melted butter.

7. Season the rolls with saffron, thyme flowers, curry powder, coriander and freshly ground black pepper. Then roll them in the mixed vegetables and smooth them with a metal spatula to obtain a fine coating.

8. In a non-stick frying pan, heat the remaining butter with the olive oil until it foams. Place the crab rolls in the pan and turn them gently until they are lightly brown. Serve three pieces per person on warm plates.

*Serve with*
***Coulée de Serrant, a strong***
***white Savennières wine.***

# .LAMB.

Star of the Easter holidays, delicious to the point of almost melting in your mouth, lamb is never more flavourful than in the spring when the grass in the meadows is tender and fresh. Spring is the time of the paschal lamb sacrificed by the Hebrew people on Easter Day in commemoration of the parting of the Red Sea.

Lamb is so called until it is one year old, at which point it becomes mutton, with tougher flesh that is flavoured slightly with a taste of wool. The best is the famous 100-day-old lamb, which is traditionally served at Easter. Though already weaned, its nourishment is based mainly on rich milk, even if it has already begun to graze. The best known are those raised in the foothills of the Alps. Their meat is very aromatic, as is that of lambs raised in the salty coastal marshes. The lambs of Poitou, Limousin, and Bordeaux also have a rich flavour.

A good lamb can be recognized by its plumpness. The meat should be white in a suckling lamb and lightly rosy, bright, with clear fat in a weaned one. The redder the meat, the closer the lamb is to adulthood.

There are three principal methods of preparing lamb: sautéing, grilling and roasting. The best parts are the saddle, the loin and the leg of lamb; it is the latter that forms the centrepiece of the traditional family feast. On the honours list of French cuisine, it remains the preferred dish. In the country of Montaigne, Rabelais and Brillat-Savarin, the lamb fan club is unrivalled.

When choosing a leg of lamb, look for one that weighs between 4–5 lb (2–2.5kg), including the bone. This way, it will be tender and flavourful. If there are many guests at table, it is better to serve two small legs of lamb rather than a larger one which may have turned to

*Nothing compares to a succulent spring lamb! Never forget that lamb must always be cooked on the bone.*

mutton. Leg of lamb must always be cooked with the bone (even if this makes it harder to cut); the flavour will be much better. Leg of lamb is usually roasted: preheat the oven to 240–270°C/475–525°F Gas Mark 9–11 or, better still, use a rotisserie or an open fireplace. Some chefs spice the lamb with garlic, but I am not in favour of this practice; I prefer to season it with chopped parsley. On the other hand, adding one or more unpeeled cloves of garlic to the bottom of the pan is advisable, along with the bones and the trimmings, for making gravy. Add all the herbs you wish: wild thyme, rosemary, basil, even cumin, as they do in North Africa. Best of all, however, is to garnish the top of the meat with sprigs of fresh thyme; its delicate aroma is the ultimate complement to lamb.

Take care never to pierce the meat, either when it is raw or in the course of cooking. Do, however, turn it often as it cooks, basting it with its own juices. Once it is cooked, it is very important to let the roast sit, covered with a sheet of aluminium foil, on the open door of the (extinguished) oven for 20 to 25 minutes. This allows the meat to relax and become tender. Add salt before cooking, though you will always need to add salt again when it comes out of the oven. Add pepper both during and after cooking. Allow 10 minutes of cooking for every lb (20 minutes per kg); lamb is generally eaten medium rare. Never very rare!

Before serving, sprinkle the top and as much of the sides as possible with a thin layer of persillade – a mixture of breadcrumbs, chopped parsley, and a pinch of finely diced garlic. Place the leg of lamb under the grill to gently brown the persillade – be very careful not to burn it. Carve the lamb along the grain, not across it. The cloves of garlic at the bottom of the pan are by now perfectly cooked, and a delicious accompaniment!

# ROAST LEG OF LAMB WITH HERBS AND SALT CRUST

1. In a food processor, combine 5 oz (150g) of coarse salt with the flour, thyme, rosemary, egg white and water. Knead in order to obtain a homogenous dough, mould it into a ball and leave to stand in the refrigerator for at least 30 minutes (overnight if possible).

2. Heat 1 teaspoon of oil in a frying pan. Add the broken bones and brown them on all sides over a high heat. Add the diced carrot, onion, celery and crushed garlic clove. Continue cooking until brown.

3. Pour off the fat and fill the pan with water. Scrape the bottom of the pan to blend in the juices and boil until the liquid has reduced to about 1 fl oz (25 ml). Strain, add the basil, cover and put aside, allowing it to steep off the heat.

4. Mix the breadcrumbs with the thyme and chopped parsley.

5. Season the lamb with salt and ground pepper; sprinkle with a mixture of breadcrumbs, thyme and parsley and roll and truss it in its fat.

6. In a bowl, prepare the glaze by

SERVES 2

1 teaspoon olive oil
1 3/4 lb (800g) loin chops, completely boned, leaving the band of fat attached at the joint; keep the broken bones.
1 carrot, diced
1 onion, diced
1 stick celery, diced
1 clove garlic, crushed
3 leaves of fresh basil
salt and ground pepper
1/3 oz (10g) fresh breadcrumbs
1 sprig of fresh thyme, leaves plucked off
1 tablespoon chopped parsley
3 1/2 fl oz (100 ml) cream
1/3 oz (10g) butter
2 egg yolks

FOR THE SALT CRUST

5 oz (150g) plus approximately 4 oz (100g) coarse sea salt
7 oz (200g) flour
6 sprigs of fresh thyme, leaves plucked
1 branch of fresh rosemary, chopped
1 egg white
3 1/2 fl oz (100 ml) water

*Serve with a robust, spicy and harmonious 1983 Château Haut-Marbuzet, Saint-Estèphe.*

mixing the egg yolks with salt and a drop of water.

7. Roll out the dough and wrap it closely around the lamb, making sure it is completely sealed. Place it in a pan in the oven.

8. Brush the surface of the dough with the glaze, sprinkle it with coarse sea salt and brush the roast a second time with the glaze.

9. Place the roast in the oven, preheated to 240°C/475°F/Gas Mark 9, for 16 minutes.

10. Finish the sauce by bringing it to a boil and adding the cream. Remove the saucepan from the heat as soon as the bubbles reduce in size. Strain, and adjust the seasoning if necessary. Add butter and whisk rapidly to emulsify the sauce.

11. Serve the lamb in its golden crust. Cut the top of the crust with a bread knife. Take out the string, pull off the fat and carve the lamb. Pour two spoonfuls of the sauce onto a warm plate, arrange the slices of lamb on the sauce, pepper with one turn of the pepper mill and serve immediately.

Roast lamb recipe, page 24.

# .VEAL.

In olden days, a veal dinner symbolized the return of the prodigal son and was featured at privileged gatherings on feast days. In modern times veal fell from favour for a while when people became concerned about hormone growth promoters. But good veal, the real thing, has come back as gourmet fare and, like lamb, is best in springtime.

Veal is the meat of a young, unweaned calf. The most succulent is milk-fed veal, which is from a calf 110 to 120 days old that has never been allowed to graze. The calf's pale pink flesh has the aroma of milk, and is as delicate and succulent as you could wish; its fat is a satiny white. It is hard to imagine such refinement when faced with row upon row of stalls of fettered calves, raised in quick succession on a diet of powdered milk, grains and vitamins bolstered with antibiotics to check frequent illnesses. Using hormones to raise veal calves is in fact forbidden. Sometimes veal calves are fed eggs, which renders their meat sublime, giving it a flavour fit for royalty. This kind of production, however, is costly and rare. You can also obtain the meat of a slightly older grass-fed calf whose flesh is darker but often tastier than the off-white meat of the pitiful calf raised in a tiny cell.

Veal must be carefully selected. Find out from your butcher its exact origins, and bear in mind that a good veal will retain its volume after cooking, as well as its delicacy. A mediocre cut of veal, on the other hand, will sometimes shrink by half when cooked. It is in fact more economical to buy a very good cut of meat. In my restaurant I serve veal from the region of Aurillac, where Raoul Fabre, a butcher devoted to his trade, has draconian procedures of selection. His meat is always of exceptional flavour and quality.

It is wise to choose the cut according to the particular recipe. For roast veal, choose the loin, sirloin or chump end, which have a more pronounced flavour.

*Veal kidneys, liver or sweetbreads must be top quality: a good indication is their colour.*

Cutlets – without the bones – are drier, except in the case of milk-fed calves of very high quality. If you have many guests, the saddle or unseparated loin may also be used, but that would be a very large roast.

In general, the small pieces are grilled or fried, and the escalope of veal remains the most classic dish. The side of the veal is taken from the loin; one thick side of veal is better for two people than two merely average cuts. The piccata is a small, very thin escalope, already trussed and ready for roasting. The paillard is a large escalope, finely flattened. The medallion or grenadin is cut from the loin. The end of the chump is like a tournedos, cut in slices around 1 inch (2.5cm) thick.

As far as entrées with a sauce are concerned, whether sautéed, braised, fricasséed or a blanquette, choose cuts that have the most marrow, such as the neck, shoulder, breast or knuckle. The latter is particularly good when poached, surrounded by new or well-braised vegetables. The offal, which is particularly sought after, has acquired the badge of honour, adorning many of the star entrées in France's top restaurants. What counts above all is freshness and quality.

Kidneys, liver or sweetbreads must be of top quality. Buy them only from the best of butchers. Colour is the criterion by which to select all cuts of veal; the lighter the offal, the higher its quality. Kidneys or livers should be a pale pink rather than deep red.

What can be said about the neglected parts of the calf? It is a mistake to ignore them, since they offer very interesting possibilities for both the palate and the purse strings. They are very inexpensive, particularly the feet and the head, which people either love or hate. Personally, I am very fond of them. For some time before I set up shop in the rue de Longchamp, I served a head of veal in a ragout which was a wild success with veal enthusiasts.

# ROLLED VEAL AND KIDNEYS

1. Remove most of the fat from the kidneys, leaving just a thin layer covering them. Add generous amounts of salt and pepper. Fry them in a bit of melted kidney fat, cooking for about 30 seconds on each side, until they are nicely browned. Season them again, and put them aside to cool.

2. Flatten the loin well, then sprinkle salt and pepper into the interior. Place the kidneys in the centre, one behind the other, and roll the meat back onto itself. Be sure to envelop the kidneys well. Tie the rolled loin with string and season the exterior.

3. Place the meat in a large casserole. Put a few knobs of butter on top, and arrange the trimmings and the pieces of bone in the bottom of the pan. Leaving the casserole uncovered, place it in the oven, which has been preheated at 260°C/500°F/Gas Mark 11. Turn every 5 or 6 minutes so that all sides of the roast will brown evenly. When the meat is well browned (approximately 30 minutes), add the aromatic garnish and then cover the casserole.

SERVES 8–10

**2 small veal kidneys**
**in their fat**
**salt and pepper**
**1 loin of veal**
**(ask the butcher**
**to remove the bones**
**and cut them, together**
**with the trimmings,**
**into small pieces)**
**butter**

FOR THE AROMATIC GARNISH
**2 carrots, sliced crosswise**
**2 onions, cut in rings**
**3 cloves garlic, whole**
**2 tomatoes, cut in quarters**
**bouquet garni of thyme,**
**snips of parsley**
**and a celery stick**

Baste the meat several times as it cooks. Time varies according to the thickness of the meat, but it should take approximately 45 minutes. Veal must be served well-done, without over-cooking it. The kidneys should stay lightly pink.

4. Once the veal is done, take it out of the oven and remove it from the casserole. Add more salt and pepper. Cover with aluminium foil, and leave to sit on the oven door for 30 minutes or so. This makes the meat more tender.

5. Place the casserole on the heat, and add 1 3/4 pt (1 litre) of water. With a wooden spoon, scrape the residues from the bottom and the sides of the pan. Allow the sauce to boil gently for 15 to 20 minutes, then skim off the surplus fat with a spoon (the sauce should remain lighty fatty) and strain.

6. Slice the meat, and place on a warm serving platter. Pour the juice into a gravy boat and serve with pasta, young vegetables or the ultimate, morels, for an ideal springtime feast.

*Serve with a 1982 Vosne-Romanée,*
*a fine and seductive wine*
*with the bouquet of ripe red fruit.*

# .BROAD BEANS.

This ancestral vegetable, originally from the Orient, has been cultivated since antiquity. We know from the Bible that among the provisions brought to David at Manahajim there was a considerable quantity of beans.

Whatever your method of cooking is to be, only use broad beans of the utmost freshness. To choose them well, you need only feel the pods to ascertain that they are full. (The pods are deceptive, since they always appear swollen even when they are empty.)

There is a wide variety of ways to cook broad beans. If they are very young, they may simply be eaten raw and seasoned with salt, as is customary in the south of France. Otherwise, they should be eaten 'naked': simply strip off the thin skin that covers them. As the season progresses, the skin grows thicker and becomes undigestible, so peeling is an absolute necessity. To do this, plunge the beans in a pot of boiling salted water – 1/2 oz (15g) of salt per 1 3/4 pt (1 litre). Count 30 seconds from boiling point, then remove the beans with a slotted spoon. If you wish to further refine the preparation, remove the sprout as well, as it gives the beans a slightly bitter flavour.

However you decide to prepare broad beans, savory will be your indispensable flavouring. The most classic recipe is the purée, but my favourite dish is savory broad bean soup. Once the beans have been peeled, cook them for about 6 minutes in boiling salted water. Strain in a colander, reserving a few of the smaller ones, which will be used as a garnish. Using

*When choosing broad beans, simply squeeze the pod.*

a fine blade, run the beans through the food processor, then place them in a large pan. In a separate saucepan, boil chicken stock and slowly pour it over the purée, stirring all the while with a whisk so that you will have a velvety soup. Add a pinch of sugar and a bouquet of savory. Bring the soup to a boil and add crème fraîche. Remove the pan from the heat and strain the soup through a fine sieve. Just before serving, gently reheat the soup until it begins to simmer, pour it into a mixing bowl and stir while adding knobs of butter. Adjust the seasoning, if necessary. Arrange the reserved beans in the bottom of the soup dish, then pour in the thick, creamy soup.

As with other pulses, broad beans may be harvested dry, but that makes the poor bean so unattractive! Its skin becomes wrinkled and its lovely green colour turns brown. Nevertheless, the dried broad bean should not be spurned. The Romans made bread from broad bean flour. In a period of scarcity, even Louis XV ate bean bread. Before haricot beans were discovered, broad beans were a staple of cassoulet. Dried beans were soaked in water, as we do with haricot beans today, and were cooked with pork, duck and sausage. In winter, try this traditional cassoulet to put a taste of spring in the air.

As with all staple foods, the broad bean has its symbolic associations. The Gallete des Rois (Kings' Cake) is eaten every year to celebrate the end of Epiphany, and contains a single dried bean representing the incarnated embryo, the germination of the life to come. The bean was also traditionally offered during the course of marriage ceremonies, and represented the yet unborn child who would perpetuate the family lineage. And, of course, is not spring a time of rebirth?

## Broad Beans and Baby Onions with Smoked Bacon

Serves 2

2 lb (1kg) broad beans,
unshelled

14 baby onions

4 oz (100g) butter

salt and ground pepper

pinch of sugar

2 oz (50g) smoked belly
of pork

pinch of fresh savory

1. Shell the beans and place them in a pan of boiling salted water. Blanch them for 30 seconds from the moment they start to boil. Refresh them, then drain them. Peel them and cook for a few more minutes in boiling salted water. Rinse and drain again.

2. Peel the onions, leaving the stem. Put them in a frying pan with a generous spoonful of butter, salt, pepper, and a pinch of sugar. Cover and gently cook over low heat, stirring from time to time. They need about 30 minutes to become golden brown and flavourful. When they are done, take the pan off the heat and set it aside.

3. Dice the smoked bacon into small pieces about about 1/16 inch (1 mm) thick. Fry them in a little butter without browning.

4. Add the onions to the bacon, followed by the beans and savory. Heat and season to taste. Serve this succulent accompaniment with offal, rabbit, poultry, or – best of all – with a young meat such as lamb.

*As for wine,*
*I recommend a spicy red Faugère*
*from Languedoc.*

Savory broad bean soup, page 32.

# .CHANTERELLES.

With tops the colour of wood, the fragile chanterelle sprouts towards the end of spring. Of the edible fungi, it is the easiest to identify. Its colour ranges from golden to pale yellow, and it has a distinctive convex trumpet-shaped cap with a frilly edge that is folded under if the mushroom is still young. The underside of the cap is garnished with fine, uneven gills which descend to a slender stem and a thick base.

This mushroom has in it all the virtues of a wild fruit. Its inimitable flavour can be guaranteed and, moreover, it has the advantage of being free to those who are willing to expend the little energy it takes to find and pick them. What a wonderful way to renew the bond with Mother Nature! Chanterelles are better in spring than in autumn. They are very much appreciated by gourmets for their firm, delicious flesh, fine apricot scent and slight acidity and bitterness.

If you buy rather than pick chanterelles, choose the little ones, which are more fragrant. The larger ones have often lost much of their quality and are sometimes rubbery. The flavour of chanterelles begins to fade only a few hours after picking, so they must be prepared as soon as possible.

Before beginning any preparation, cut off the base of the mushroom. Rinse thoroughly under running water, checking to be sure that there is no debris attached to the cap. Do not soak them as they will absorb water, which will dilute their flavour and make cooking more difficult. Next, boil a large pan of salted water,

*Slightly acidic and a little bitter, June's chanterelles are delicious.*

plunge in the mushrooms, and then take them out immediately. Drain. This operation makes the surface of the mushroom contract, seals in its flavour, fixes its colour and preserves its texture. This way, they will release less water when they are cooked.

The standard way to prepare chanterelles is to sauté them. To do this, finely chop a shallot, place it in a frying pan with a knob of butter and a pinch of salt, and sweat it over a low heat – without allowing it to brown – until it is translucent. Remove the shallot and put it aside. Next, heat the butter to foaming and add the chanterelles, which have been lightly blanched in boiling salted water and drained. Do not add salt right away, or the mushrooms will release their liquid. Sauté them for a few minutes, then add the cooked shallot. Season and add chopped parsley or chervil to taste. I do not recommend adding garlic, since it robs the mushroom of its delicate taste; if you are a great fan of garlic, it is best to rub the frying pan with a clove beforehand. Chanterelles go equally well with delicate flavours such as crème fraîche and strongly flavoured dishes like game. They may also be eaten raw, marinated in a herb vinaigrette. I actually prefer them cooked, as this fibrous mushroom, often leathery when raw, can be indigestible if eaten uncooked. Cooked chanterelles are a perfect accompaniment to chicken, veal, steak, hare, offal, eggs, and even fish or shellfish. They bring a touch of their own inimitable flavour to any dish.

# FRICASSÉE OF CHANTERELLES WITH WILD ASPARAGUS

1. Bring the chicken stock to a boil. Add the chanterelles, and allow them to boil only briefly. Remove the chanterelles with a slotted spoon, reserving the chicken stock. It will be used for the sauce and the dressing for the asparagus.

2. Thinly slice the button mushrooms. Place the butter and the chopped onion in a pan with a pinch of salt. As soon as the onion becomes translucent, add the sliced mushrooms and sweat them without letting them brown. Stir well, then add the boiling chicken stock, making sure to reserve 3 tablespoons for the asparagus. Add the bouquet garni, cover, and simmer over low heat for 20 minutes.

3. Run the mixture through the food processor, then strain. Place the saucepan back on the heat, adding two-thirds of the cream. Add a tablespoon of water to the cornflour, and use it to thicken the mushroom cream sauce. Put the sauce through the food processor again.

4. Put the finely chopped shallot in a small saucepan with a tablespoon of butter and a pinch

**SERVES 6**

**14oz–1 1/4 lb (400–500 g) small chanterelles, washed**

**1 shallot, finely chopped**

**3 oz (75g) butter**

**salt and pepper**

**30 small wild asparagus spears**

**chopped chervil,**

FOR THE MUSHROOM CREAM SAUCE

**1/2 pint (300 ml) chicken stock**

**11 oz (300 g) button mushrooms, washed**

**3/4 oz (20g) butter**

**1/2 small onion, chopped**

**salt and pepper**

**1 bouquet garni**

**2 fl oz (50 ml) cream**

**1/3 oz (10g) cornflour**

**tabasco sauce**

of salt. Heat until translucent, then remove the saucepan from the heat. Set it aside for a moment.

5. Cook the asparagus in boiling salted water. Rinse and strain. Allow to cool.

6. To finish, reheat the mushroom cream sauce and add the remaining cream. Season with salt, pepper and a dash of tabasco sauce.

7. Melt 1 1/2 oz (40 g) of butter in a non-stick pan. Add the chanterelles. Toss in the cooked shallot and cook for 2 minutes, stirring constantly. Season and add the chopped chervil.

8. Arrange the asparagus in a small frying pan. Prepare a butter sauce with 1 1/4 oz (30 g) of butter and the reserved 3 tablespoons of chicken stock. Pour over the asparagus and gently turn them in the pan as they reheat. Season.

9. To serve, distribute the chanterelles in the centre of the plate and arrange the asparagus on top. Blend the mushroom cream sauce one more time in the food processor and pour around the plate.

*Serve with a full-bodied Tokay pinot gris from Alsace.*

# .CARROTS.

Who hasn't stood on the edge of a field or forest and admired the little umbels of wild carrots swaying gracefully among the tall grass and wild herbs? Their feathery, branching stems are quite tall, supporting finely cut leaves and clusters of minuscule red or white flowers, spread like umbrellas, from which comes their family name: Umbelliferae. This wild vegetable is the parent of the cultivated carrot.

*The best way to prepare new carrots is to glaze them – an exquisite recipe.*

Until the Renaissance, the carrot was just a simple root. Tough, white, with a fibrous heart, it went unappreciated, excluded from the company of more noble vegetables. Thanks to crossbreeding, which began in the last century, the carrot became the flavoursome and colourful vegetable so popular today.

The carrot has a tender flavour that is one of spring's delights. Since the era of Hippocrates and Dioscorides Pedanius, numerous medicinal benefits have also been attributed to it. Its richness in carotene in the form of provitamin-A promotes growth, improves night vision, and helps blood regenerate by increasing its haemoglobin content. It supplies minerals, firms skin tissues and is a renowned anti-wrinkle agent. Because of its high fibre content, it possesses important dietetic properties. It is even said that eating carrots makes one more attractive, probably due to the good complexion they provide.

There are many varieties of carrot. The small and tender new carrots of spring are much better than tinned ones. Carrots from Créances (in the Manche region) deserve special mention: they are sold with a label certifying the place of production, and describing the quality of the cultivation – the carrots are protected while they grow by a blanket of hay, heather, gorse or seaweed.

The rule of thumb for choosing good carrots is generally that the more orange they are, the sweeter. They should be tender, with a fine, smooth surface, uniform in colour, without spots, and the tops should be firmly attached. A split carrot is a sure sign that it has stayed in the ground for too long, and has therefore lost its best qualities.

Contrary to popular belief, which holds it to be a drab, monotonous vegetable, the carrot can be prepared in an incredible range of ways, which allows it to cater for the greatest of gourmet pleasures. Raw and grated, the sugary carrot marries well with the acidity of lemon, olive oil, and a pinch of garlic, which gives it its personality. Try it also with walnuts, hazelnuts, pulped fruit or olive oils. It also goes well with almonds, pinenuts and steamed raisins, not to mention the plant of the devil – parsley.

Carrot juice makes for famously healthy cocktails; it also goes very well with tomatoes. Lemon juice complements the carrot's flavour and enhances the colour. Other flavour-boosters include celery, fennel, garlic, onion, shallots, and the ever-wonderful ginger, in small quantities.

Once cooked, carrots marry well with everything that might need a sweet note. They are wonderful with orange juice, wild herbs, thyme, basil, tarragon, sage, and mint, so long as they are used sparingly, allowing the flavours to mingle with rather than dominate the carrot's delicate aroma. I have a fondness for fresh coriander and cumin, which bring an oriental note to the carrot.

In my opinion, the best way to prepare new carrots is to glaze them, an exquisite recipe. Peel them with a knife rather than scraping them; they are much prettier that way. If they are especially large, cut them in half, but do not make the common error of turning them as if they were potatoes, which takes off the most delicate part. Place them in as large a saucepan as possible and cover them with water. Add a little salt, 2 1/4 oz (60g) of butter and 1 1/4 oz (30g) of sugar for 18 fl oz (500 ml) of water. Place a paper towel soaked in melted butter over the carrots and fold so that it just fits. Place the saucepan over medium heat. Thanks to this improvised cover, the water evaporates little by little, and the carrots are done when the water has fully evaporated. The carrots will be barely coloured, glazed with butter and sugar, and ready to melt in your mouth.

# CARROTS WITH CUMIN

SERVES 4

1 3/4 lb (800g)
new carrots

salt

1 clove garlic,
finely chopped

1 teaspoon sugar

1/3 oz (10g) cumin

2 tablespoons olive oil

1 bouquet garni, made
of parsley stalks,
a stick of celery,
a sprig of thyme and a sprig
of fresh coriander

1 teaspoon (5g) butter

juice of 3 oranges

1. Peel the carrots and slice them into thin rounds.

2. Place them in a large bowl. Salt them, then add the garlic, sugar, cumin and olive oil. Mix thoroughly.

3. Place the mixture in as large a saucepan as possible and fill it half full with water. Add the bouquet garni. Place a paper towel soaked in butter over the carrots; pierce it with a few holes so as to allow the steam to escape.

4. Bring to the boil, then reduce to medium heat for 25 minutes.

5. Take the paper towel off and remove the bouquet garni. Add the orange juice and finish cooking over low heat until all the liquid has evaporated, stirring around the edge of the pot so that the olive oil and sugar are well distributed and the glaze is shiny and uniform.

*Serve with a white wine
from Provence; Château Simone
is pleasant and full.*

# .CHERRIES.

One of spring's highlights is the all-too-brief cherry season. The succulent fruit of the cherry tree, whose magnificent white flowers are in bloom at the beginning of spring, is harvested from mid-May to the beginning of July. We all have early childhood memories of cherries adorning our ears, so they bring with them reminders of our first desires and pleasures.

Cherries are the offspring of two primitive families; the wild sweet cherry tree and the bitter cherry tree. The most common sweet cherry is the bigarreau, of which there are a number of varieties. These fruit are round, deep red, sometimes black, firm and sweet-smelling. The juicy little gean cherry is mostly used for kirsch and liqueurs. Bitter or sour cherries are smaller. They are slightly softer, and are either purple or vermilion. The best-known are the morello and the famous short-stemmed Montmorency cherry. This succulent little cherry with a translucent skin gave birth to that classic of French cuisine, Montmorency duck. When macerated in vinegar, they are the ideal accompaniment for game. They also go well in eau-de-vie.

When buying cherries, choose pretty ones with smooth shiny skin and a bright colour; avoid those that are overripe or spotted. The stem should be a bold green colour, supple and firmly attached. Cherries, like most red fruit, are delicate and must be handled with care in transport; they do not like heat or stormy weather.

Cherries may be kept for up to two or three days in the refrigerator, but do not eat them cold as their flavour will be diminished. They should be washed with the stem still attached, and may be eaten raw or cooked.

*Whether bigarreau, little gean or morello, spring is the time for cherries.*

Here is a recipe for an excellent cherry sauce. Remove the stones from 1 1/4 lb (500g) of morello or Montmorency cherries. If you do not have a stoner, puncture the ends with a hairpin or a paperclip broken in two with the ends anchored in a cork. Remove the stones without bruising the flesh and, above all, without losing any of the juice. Heat 18 fl oz (500 ml) of red wine, 3 1/2 fl oz (100 ml) of vinaigrette and about 2 fl oz (50ml) of sherry in a pan. When it boils, add 2 oz (50g) of sugar and the cherries with their juice. Bring back to the boil and remove from the heat immediately. Cover and allow to cool. Once the saucepan is lukewarm, remove the cherries. Place the remaining juice back on the heat to reduce until it is of a syrupy consistency. Add the syrup to the juices of cooked meat and place the cherries back in this bittersweet sauce. This sauce may be served cold, accompanied by cold chicken in aspic.

Cherries are at their best in desserts – plain, of course. But they must be savoured in small quantities and without drinking – because cherries are rich in cellulose, they absorb liquid and can become indigestible. They are also delicious in fruit salad, stewed, with ice cream, in mousse, soup and jam. Even better than such sweets as Black Forest gâteau and cherry tarts is clafoutis – baked cherry custard – which really makes the most of the cherry. Then there are glacé cherries, the indispensable ingredient for cakes and certain cocktails. And, rather than discarding the cherry stems, try them in an infusion: they make a very efficient diuretic.

449.

# CHERRY GRATIN

**SERVES 4**

**1 3/4 lb (800g) cherries**

**1 1/4 oz (30g) butter**

**3 1/4 oz (80g) caster sugar**

**1 tablespoon kirsch**

**3 egg yolks**

**3 1/2 fl oz (100 ml) white wine**

**5 oz (150g) cream, well chilled**

1. Wash and stone the cherries and remove the stems. In a pot, place 1 1/4 oz (30g) of butter, 1 1/2 oz (40g) of caster sugar and the cherries with their juice. Cover and bring the mixture to a boil for 3 minutes. Remove the lid, add the kirsch and flambé the cherries. Cover again and remove from the heat; set aside to cool.

2. In a small bowl, combine the 3 egg yolks, the white wine, and the rest of the caster sugar to make a sabayon.

3. Place the bowl in a pan of simmering water, as you would for a bain-marie. Using an electric mixer, blend the sabayon into a fine froth until it is at least four times its original volume. Take the sabayon off the heat and let it cool.

4. Whip the cream and stir it gently into the sabayon.

5. Strain the cherries with a slotted spoon and arrange them in a porcelain flan dish. Cover them copiously with sabayon.

6. Place the gratin under the grill until the top is lightly browned.

*Serve*
*with a cold pink*
*champagne.*

# .STRAWBERRIES.

It was not until the 15th century that cultivation of the wild strawberry began. Strawberries do not have a real country of origin; they are universal. And it is in the heart of spring that nature makes a gift of this exquisite fruit.

This gourmet's delicacy is said to have aphrodisiacal qualities. With its pretty red dress, voluptuous curves, sugary perfume and sweet astringency, the strawberry is the star of all fruit during the month of May.

Today, strawberries may be found year-round in many countries, which offends the sensibilities of gourmets. Let us stay faithful to the season and the beautiful weather in which the delicious French strawberry grows. Among numerous varieties, the most flavourful are the very red Pajaro, which is shaped like a conical heart, the Galbée Elsanta, with its firm flesh and unique aroma, and the Garriguette, which is gracefully elongated, meltingly sweet and juicy. Whatever your choice, do not buy your strawberries more than 48 hours in advance. They turn rot-

*With its pretty red dress, voluptuous curves and sugary perfume, nothing is more appetizing than the strawberry.*

ten without warning. Like cherries, strawberries are fragile and dislike heat and stormy weather.

Choose fresh, ripe and healthy strawberries, and savour them as soon as you buy them. Quality is not at all a matter of size. Large, good-looking fruit often turns out to be tasteless. Good strawberries are bright red, the stem is green and rigid and the skin should be neither split nor bruised. The tip should also be coloured, which is a sign of ripeness. A dull colour indicates that it has been kept too long; if green, the strawberry will never ripen.

If they must be stored, keep them in their original package and place them in the bottom drawer of the refrigerator. Avoid handling them. Wash them by rinsing a few at a time under cold running water (do not hull them first as they will absorb water and lose their flavour). After washing, hull them and prepare them immediately.

Plain, with a fine dusting of sugar, under a blanket of cream or a cloud of whipped cream – there are unlimited ways to savour the strawberry. Some gourmets prefer them steeped in lemon juice or embellished with just a hint of wine vinegar, kirsch, champagne, wine, etc. Strawberries are wonderful in salads, as well as in tarts, mousses, soufflés, bavarois and a wide array of sweets. Mix them with a little sugar and a squeeze of lemon to obtain a wonderful coulis, or sauce. Take advantage of the last moments before the markets close, when sweet-smelling strawberries are still abundant, to find bargains.

You might also consider making an easy sorbet, such as the following: wash, drain and hull 2 lb (1kg) of strawberries. Blend them in a food processor, then add 7 oz (200g) of icing sugar and the juice of half a lemon and blend again. Pass through a sieve, using a ladle to push the pulp through. Churn in an ice-cream maker. Serve when the sorbet is still soft. If you do not like sorbet, you could make jam – raw or cooked, strawberries are enchanting.

## STRAWBERRY SOUP

SERVES 4

**1 1/4 lb (500g) ripe
strawberries**

**1 teaspoon wine vinegar**

**4 oz (100g) caster sugar**

**2 lemons**

**7 fl oz (200ml) orange juice**

**1 1/2 fl oz (50ml)
orange-flower water**

1. Wash and quarter the strawberries. Add the wine vinegar and half the caster sugar. Let them marinate in the refrigerator for 1 hour.

2. Wash the lemons and pare them with a knife. Cut the peel into a fine julienne, and put in a pan. Cover with cold water. Bring to a boil, drain, then refresh with cold water.

3. Return the lemon julienne to the pan, add the rest of the sugar, and 3 1/2 fl oz (100 ml) of water. Cook over a low heat for about 20 minutes, until the lemon is crystallized, then set it aside.

4. After 1 hour add the orange juice and orange-flower water to the strawberries. Mix well and place them in pretty glass bowls. Top with the julienne of candied lemon peel and serve chilled.

*Serve with a golden Muscat
de Beaumes-de-Venise.*

# .APRICOTS.

A fruit with pretty velvety golden skin the colour of the sun and delicate, sweet-smelling flesh, the apricot is pure delight. This golden fruit grows on small ornamental trees in orchards.

Chinese in origin, the apricot appeared in France in the 15th century and was originally cultivated in Roussillon. There are only a few varieties grown. The first apricots of the season ripen at the end of May, the latest in August.

Try to buy home-grown apricots rather than imports, which tend to be bland. A good apricot should not be too big, and should be fresh and perfectly ripe. Once it has been picked it will not ripen further, so if it is harvested too early it will gain neither flavour nor fragrance and its flesh will be woolly rather than juicy and astringent. Look for apricots that are plump, tender to the touch without being soft, thin-skinned, slightly downy, well-coloured and unbruised. Ah, there is nothing to match the flavour of a perfectly ripe apricot!

Be very cautious when handling apricots, for they are a fragile fruit. Storing them too long will make them bland and mealy. They may be eaten plain. Remove them from the refrigerator well before you intend to use them in order to appreciate their sweetness. Rinse them under running water without letting them soak, and dry them carefully.

Apricots are one of the most popular fruits for preserves, and this is their main commercial use. Making them into preserves allows the fruits that are too small and underripe for the greengrocers to be used instead of wasted.

If you make preserve yourself, don't forget to put in a few of the kernels from the apricot stones. They give a delicious flavour. Use them also in an apricot compote. Wrap them in a piece of muslin or fine linen and tie it into a little bag. Cut the apricots in two, remove the stones and extract the kernels to add to the muslin bag. Next,

*Here is a tart that celebrates the most golden of fruit.*

prepare a syrup with 12 oz (350 g) of sugar per 1 3/4 pt (1 litre) of water and a vanilla pod. Let the sugar dissolve and boil for 1 or 2 minutes after you have added the bag of kernels. Carefully skim off any impurities that rise to the surface. As soon as the syrup bubbles, add the apricots, submerge them well, and let them simmer on low heat, without allowing the mixture to boil. Gently poach the fruit for about 10 minutes, then allow to cool in the pan. Strain them, then mix in some well-ripened apricots and pass through a sieve. Thin the resulting pulp with some of the juice left over from the cooking. To finish, pour the sauce over the fruit and decorate with a few fresh blanched kernels and mint leaves.

But it is apricot tart that truly celebrates this fruit. Line a pie dish with puff pastry and pierce the pastry with a fork. Bake the pastry blind. To do this, cover the pastry shell with aluminium foil and place beans on the base (unless you prefer the old-fashioned way using scrubbed pebbles) and bake it for 7 or 8 minutes in the oven at 230°C/450°F/Gas Mark 8. Then remove the weights and aluminum foil and return the pastry shell to the oven to bake uncovered for another 5 minutes. In the meantime, prepare the almond cream. With a wooden spatula, combine 2 oz (50g) of butter with an equal portion of icing sugar. Then add 2 oz (50g) of ground almonds. Mix well and add a whole egg. Mix again and place in the refrigerator for 10 minutes. Cut the apricots in two, removing the stones. Take the pastry shell and cover it with the almond cream so that the juice of the apricots will not seep into the pastry during cooking. If you do not like almond cream, you may use a very fine layer of crushed biscuits or a very fine wheat flour, which will absorb the fruit juice and keep the crust from becoming soggy. Arrange the apricots in concentric circles cut side uppermost so that the juice will stay in the centre of the fruit rather than run down onto the crust. Bake the tart for about 45 minutes at 220°C/425°F/Gas Mark 7. After removing it from the oven, sprinkle the tart with icing sugar. The apricot is one of the most popular fruits for any number of desserts and pastries.

## Apricot Upside-down Tart

Serves 6

2 1/2 lb (1.2 kg) ripe apricots

11 oz (300g) puff pastry

3 1/4 oz (80g) fresh butter

2 1/4 oz (60g) caster sugar

2 oz (50g) icing sugar

1. Wash the apricots, cut them in two and remove the stones.

2. Roll out the puff pastry to obtain an 8 1/2 inch (22 cm) diameter crust that is approximately 1 1/4 inches (3cm) thick.

3. Take a frying pan or, better, a chafing dish that will go in the oven. Combine the butter and the caster sugar and heat until it becomes golden.

4. Remove the pan from the heat and leave to cool.

5. Arrange the apricots side by side in concentric circles cut side uppermost in the bottom of the pan.

6. Cover with a lid of pastry that is slightly bigger than the surface area and put the tart in the oven at 230°C/450°F/Gas Mark 8. Cook for about 20 minutes. Leave to cool completely.

7. To turn out the tart, heat the pan gently on the stove; the apricots should then be easily detached.

8. Sprinkle the apricots with icing sugar and place the tart briefly under the grill to caramelize it.

*Serve immediately with a fresh liqueur-like wine such as a Muscat de Rivesaltes.*

# .VANILLA.

Vanilla is the gourmet's goddess. The pod studded with perfumed grains is the fruit of the vanilla plant (Vanilla plonifolia) of the orchid family. This tropical plant with greenish-white blooms was once a mere parasite of the larger trees of Central America. Today, vanilla is cultivated in Madagascar, Tahiti, the West Indies, and on many isles of the Indian Ocean. The most popular and highly regarded vanilla comes from La Réunion, once called Bourbon, hence the name Bourbon vanilla.

Without pollinating insects, the cultivation of vanilla was, at the beginning, very difficult. The stroke of genius was the development of manual fertilization, in which a thorn is used to put the male and female elements of the flower into contact. It takes four or five years before a stalk of vanilla delivers its first blooms. In addition, it is only fertile in the first five hours following the appearance of the blooms. Needless to say, vanilla growers must move quickly, and spend from 6am to noon in the fields. It then takes one year for the fertilized flower to yield a pod of ripe vanilla, which looks like a large French bean. The pod takes another year to acquire its aroma and undergo a complex commercial maturation process which includes a three-minute scalding in water at 150°F (65°C), one night covered by wool (which makes the bean turn brown) and six or seven one-hour sessions in an oven, which takes a week. This is followed by one week of exposure to the sun for one hour per day. To develop the aroma, growers put the pods in hermetically sealed bins for 12 months. A good vanilla specialist will always be able to recognize the provenance of the bean and even its producer: while green the pods are stamped with an identifying sign that is distinguishable even after preparation.

The aroma of vanilla is so intoxicating that, if inhaled in large quantities, it has the effect of a mild drug. Drugged on vanilla, who would ever have believed it? The richest aroma of all is that of frosted vanilla: the pods are partially covered with a white frost, which is not mould but crystals of vanilla condensation. These crystals are the surplus that exudes from the skin of the pod during compression. Naturally rare, this is the

*The* **nec plus ultra** *is the frosted vanilla pod,* **nature's** **grand cru.**

*grand cru* of vanillas; it is what I order directly from the cooperative in the Bras-Paon, which only produces 110 lb (50 kg) per year, out of a total annual production of about 150 tons!

Vanilla is the sweet flavouring which is loved the world round. Its uses are many, and it has been honoured by many famous chefs. It likewise figures in the distillation of certain drinks. However, vanilla is at its most noble in pastries and candies.

The most classic preparation is *crème anglaise à la vanille*. It is not an easy recipe and the amateur *cordon bleu* cook could fail with it. Its smoothness comes from the coagulation of the egg yolks when heated. The more eggs you put in, the thicker and smoother it will be. Allow 10 or 12 egg yolks for every 1 3/4 pt (1 litre) of milk and 9 oz (250g) of caster sugar.

To make *crème anglaise*, fill a large pan with cold water, pour out the water without drying the pan, then put the milk in the pan. This way, the milk will not stick to the bottom and the sides of the pan as it cooks. Cut three pods of vanilla lengthwise. Scrape the interiors with a knife, put the contents with a single coffee bean in 1 3/4 pt (1 litre) of milk and bring to a boil. Cover and let it steep for 5 or 10 minutes. Meanwhile, pour the sugar into a bowl. Make a small well in the middle and add 12 egg yolks. Whisk immediately with an electric beater to obtain a smooth mixture that is foamy and double in volume. There is no such thing as too much mixing! As a matter of hygiene, it is a good idea to wash your hands after breaking the eggs since the shells may carry disease, especially if the eggs are from a farm. Once the eggs and sugar mixture is foamy, pour in two ladles of hot milk. Stir in carefully, then pour the mixture into the pan with the rest of the milk, whisking well. Put the pan over a low heat and stir constantly and gently with a wooden spatula. This is the delicate part of the operation. The cream should thicken but it should not cook too much; it should never boil. If it does, it will turn lumpy due to setting of the egg yolks. The ideal temperature is about 185°F (85°C). To determine exactly when it is ready, press your finger

on the spatula. If the imprint stays well-marked, the custard is ready; if the edges spread out and then flow back together, it is not. Strain the custard through a fine sieve into an unheated porcelain dish and, if possible, place the dish in a bowl of iced water so as to stop the cooking process and cool the mixture quickly. This custard is extremely delicate. It should be made with top-quality ingredients and eaten within hours after its preparation, otherwise it may become toxic.

Be careful! With farm eggs and raw milk (if you can find it), it will have all the more flavour, but since the milk will not have been pasteurized, the custard will be even more delicate.

One of the best vanilla desserts is the Caramelized Custard with Brown Sugar. One important detail: do not reduce the proportions recommended here, because a certain quantity is necessary for the recipe to turn out correctly.

# CARAMELIZED CUSTARD WITH BROWN SUGAR

SERVES 8

**3 vanilla pods**

**7 eggs**

**5 oz (150g) caster sugar**

**8 fl oz (250 ml) milk**

**1 1/4 pt (750 ml) top-quality double cream**

**1 tablespoon brown sugar**

1. Cut the vanilla pods in half lengthwise. With the point of a knife, pull the seeds out and put them in a bowl with 7 egg yolks.

2. Add the sugar and whisk until the mixture becomes slightly foamy.

3. Add the milk and cream. Whisk well, detaching any vanilla grains that stick to the sides of the bowl.

4. Pass through a fine sieve. Skim the surface.

5. Fill shallow porcelain bowls. The thickness of the custard should not exceed 3/4 inches (1.5 cm).

6. Place the bowls in an oven preheated to 170°C/325°F/Gas Mark 3 for 25 minutes. The custard should thicken, yet tremble gently when done. Take the dishes out of the oven and place them in the refrigerator.

7. Sift the brown sugar over the surface of the chilled custard.

8. Caramelize the custards lightly under the grill, then return them to the refrigerator for 10 minutes.

*Serve with a chilled Muscat de Beaumes-de-Venise.*

SUMMER

# .BREAD.

Nourishment par excellence, bread is a generous gift from Nature. This staff of life, full of symbolism, is part of the great epicurean triad, along with olive oil and wine. Mmmm – that wonderful aroma of bread baking in the ovens of the boulangerie always evokes memories and emotions!

The art of making bread goes back centuries. Bread such as is known today was born in the time of Hammurabi, King of Babylon, who published a list of foods which included bread and barley beer, drawn from the same basic thick gruel, which fermented spontaneously. This was probably the origin of the first leavening agent. But it was the Egyptians who discovered that wheat flour, left to rise with a barley yeast, was the most suitable for making bread. In any case, until Pasteur discovered microorganisms, it was simply established without explanation that the dough expanded and puffed up, and gave the impression that it was alive. Little by little, this dough replaced gruel and biscuits. Nevertheless, some peoples continue to subsist on biscuits made of millet, buckwheat, rye and other grains.

Bread accompanies the most important events in our lives, from birth to death. Certain holidays are marked by the consumption of special breads. From the death of the grain to its resurrection as an ear of wheat, from its torture in the mill to its sacrifice in the course of the meal, bread incarnates the cycle of life.

Wheat bread reunites the four indispensable elements of life: the earth, where the wheat grain takes root, develops and grows; water, that indispensable element without which the flour would remain inert and crude; air, for the fermentation, transformation and 'life' of the dough; and fire, or heat, which determines the baking of the shaped loaf.

All the senses are influenced by bread: its pleasing golden colour, its wonderful aroma, its crispness to the touch, the crackling sound it makes when it is taken out of the oven and, most of all, its inimitable taste.

*From the death of the grain to its resurrection as an ear of wheat, from its torture in the mill to its sacrifice in the course of the meal, bread incarnates the cycle of life.*

Bread is also the symbol of solidarity. The sharing of bread is one of the most positive aspects of community among people. The first petition in the Catholic oration is 'Give us today our daily bread' and without going back to the Last Supper, the word *compain* in old French, which became *copain*, or 'companion' signified sharing the same ration of bread. This is also the etymology of *compagne*, *compagnon* and *compagnonnage* (trade-guild). And there is the popular French expression *Bon comme pain* (literally, good as bread), meaning that something is extremely good; *avoir du pain sur la planche* or 'having a lot of bread on one's plate', to mean that one has a large task ahead; *manger son pain blanc* or 'to eat one's bread white', meaning to be in an advantageous situation…

There has long been a debate as to whether eating bread causes weight gain. The opinion of doctors and nutritionists has changed considerably in recent years. Eliminating bread from one's diet as a means of losing weight is not recommended, indeed the contrary: the notion that bread is an element of a healthy diet, and ally of certain diets, has been confirmed.

Baking your own bread is quite feasible. For centuries, throughout the French countryside, the woman of the house was expected to do so. Baking your own bread brings much personal satisfaction. The essential part is the rising. I cannot close without a personal reminiscence of my childhood. In my family, there was no question that bread could not be sliced without first tracing a cross upon its surface with the point of a knife. Then, bread was highly respected. The image of our mother holding the loaf against her breast as she sliced the bread for everyone gave the impression that we were not just receiving bread, but daily sustenance from she who had given us life.

# BREAD

### LEAVENED DOUGH

1. Put the raisins in a bowl with 1/4 pt (150 ml) of water and set aside in a warm place until the water begins to ferment: a white film will rise to the surface.

2. Run the water through a fine cloth and wring it well to get the maximum yeast; mix the water obtained with 5 oz (150g) of the wheat flour to obtain a soft roll. Knead and shape the dough into a ball and leave it to rise in a covered glass bowl at room temperature (about 68°F/20°C) .

3. After 1 or 2 days, sometimes more, the yeast begins to work, which may be easily seen through the bowl.

4. When the dough has tripled in volume, add 2 oz (50g) of the flour and 1 fl oz (25 ml) of water to the bowl, folding these ingredients into the dough.

5. Set the bowl aside again and wait for a second rising.

### KNEADING

1. Mix the remaining flour (1 lb 13 oz/900g) in the bowl of an electric mixer with the remaining water (about 3/4 pt/450ml), until the dough is neither too firm nor too soft. Continue mixing slowly for about 7 or 8 minutes.

2. Cover the mixing bowl and leave for 20 minutes.

3. Next, add the baker's yeast, the salt and the dough. The temperature of the dough should be roughly 68°F (20°C), or room temperature. Knead the dough slowly for 8 minutes.

3/4 oz (20g) raisins

1 pt (600 ml) water

2 1/4 lb (1.1 kg) plain flour

1 g baker's yeast

1/2 oz (15g) salt

4. Cover the bowl and allow the dough to rise until it has tripled in volume.

### CHECKING THE DOUGH

Knock down the dough and allow it to rise a second time. The dough, which should always remain at room temperature, should now be ready for shaping.

### SHAPING AND BAKING

1. Lightly flour a work surface, and shape the dough into loaves according to your needs. A good size is about 9 oz (250 g) each.

2. Gently shape the dough either in balls or in elongated shapes, being careful not to overknead the dough.

3. Put the shaped loaves on a clean cloth, not too close together. Cover the loaves with another cloth so that they will not dry up.

4. When the loaves have tripled in volume, transfer them onto a baking sheet, using a small planchette or elongated spatula.

5. With a razor blade, make a 1/2 inch (1 cm) incision along the top of the loaf.

6. Place the sheet in an oven that has been preheated to 475°F/250°C/Gas Mark 9 and humidified with a pan full of boiling water.

7. Baking time is approximately 35 minutes.

Note: By reserving about 2 oz (50 g) of leavened dough from time to time, it is possible to use it as a base for dough rather than having to start once again from scratch.

# .HARICOT BEANS.

The fresh French bean, that spindly summer vegetable with a tender smooth dress, is a gift from the New World, introduced to our continent in the 16th century.

For the gourmet, the French bean is irreplaceable if it is savoured in the right season: summertime. French beans grown in country gardens are often better than those imported from foreign tropical climes such as Kenya, though those are often also excellent. This is a fragile vegetable that often suffers during shipping.

Though you should be able to find them year round, the remarkable subtlety of the French bean is lost if it is not fresh. Nothing tastes better than a French bean picked that same day. To judge its quality, bend it: it should break crisply and cleanly. Choose healthy, thin beans, all of the same size.

French beans must be washed in plenty of water then drained in a colander. If they are not indisputably fresh, if they have begun to fade even slightly, let them soak for about an hour and they will become crisp again. By washing them before trimming, the beans will absorb less water. When trimming, do so carefully in order to remove the tops and tails and all the strings.

French beans must be cooked with care to preserve their flavour. Boil a large quantity of water, three times the volume of beans (the more water you use, the better they will be). Do not use an aluminium saucepan or casserole because the beans will blacken. Copper pots are ideal, since they enhance the colour of the beans. To preserve their green colour, salt the water generously: for about 4 oz (100g) of beans, allow 1 3/4 pt (1 litre) of water and about 1/2 oz (15g) of coarse salt. The first time you cook French beans, measure the water and weigh the salt so that you become familiar with the proportions. Do not add salt until the water has begun to boil, since salt accelerates the boiling of water. It is at this precise moment that you should add the beans: stir them well and, most importantly, make sure the water keeps boiling. Do not cover the pan, as

*Seven golden rules*

*for fabulous*

*French beans,*

*with or without ice!*

doing so will cause the beans to blacken.

The cooking time varies according to the size of the beans, so do not rely too heavily on the timer. Taste the beans regularly: they should stay firm, but not too much so. Once they are cooked, you have two options, depending on when the beans will be served. Whether you serve them immediately – which is always preferable but not always convenient – or keep them, do not pour them directly into a colander; remove them from the pan with a slotted spoon so that any impurities will not stick to the beans.

If the beans are to be eaten immediately, add butter, and allow it to melt over the vegetable, English style. On the other hand, if they are prepared in advance, take them out of the pan and place them in a bowl of ice-cold water so that they cool as rapidly as possible, preserving their colour and consistency. Then drain them as quickly as possible. Do not rinse them under running water, which will denature them. And, most of all, do not try to create a short cut by adding cold water to the water in which the beans were cooked; they will not cool fast enough this way. All these may seem to be simple details, but good cooking is made up of precisely that.

To reheat the beans before serving, simply cook them for 1 minute in a pan of boiling salted water, then drain. To prepare them, do not melt butter in a frying pan or saucepan before adding it to the vegetables. Butter should be added fresh and unmelted, unless you would like to fry the beans and add a squeeze of lemon, shallots, garlic, parsley, etc.

Here are the seven commandments for preparing French beans: 1. Use a lot of water 2. Salt well. 3. Cook the beans in boiling water. 4. Do not cover the pan. 5. Use a slotted spoon to remove the beans. 6. Drain them well. 7. Cool them rapidly in iced water if you are not going to serve them immediately. James de Coquet, the eminent author of *Propos de Table*, underlines an eternal principle: 'Between the moment when the French beans are not cooked enough and the moment when they are overcooked there is but a flicker of the eyelashes. That is where cooking and history meet. Sometimes it takes the tiniest of things to change its course.'

## FRENCH BEAN SALAD
## WITH CREAM

**SERVES 4**

**1 1/2 lb (600g) French beans**

**4 white button mushrooms**

**salt and ground pepper**

**juice of 1 lemon**

**3 1/2 fl oz (100 ml) crème
fraîche**

**1 diced shallot**

**1 tablespoon finely chopped
parsley**

1. Wash the beans, top and tail them, and remove the strings.

2. Put the beans into boiling salted water, allowing them to cook uncovered at a high boil. While they are still firm, remove them with a slotted spoon and plunge them in very cold water, then drain.

3. Wash and julienne the mushrooms.

4. Put salt and ground pepper in a salad bowl. Add the lemon juice, the crème fraîche, chopped shallot and parsley. Mix them well with a whisk.

5. Add the drained beans and the julienned mushrooms and toss well.

*Serve with*
*a chilled*
*white Sancerre.*

# .Mussels.

It is during the wheat and maize season that this delicious seafood appears at its best. Wild mussel beds stretch all along the French coast, but these mussels are smaller and less tasty than those that have been cultivated.

Since good things often happen by chance, the cultivation of mussels is linked to a shipwreck. In 1735, an Irish navigator's ship ran aground in the bay of L'Aiguillon. He drove in stakes and stretched out nets in hopes of capturing the birds that skimmed the surface of the water at night. He then discovered that the submerged wood bore colonies of mussels that were plumper and more savoury than those of the wild variety. And thus was born the *bouchot*, or mussel farm, which derives from two words that are Celtic in origin, *bout* (enclosure) and *chaos* (wood). Patrick Walton therefore became the first mussel farmer on French soil. For a long time, his method was the only one practised in France. Cultivation *à plat*, or flat, originated in Holland, and 'suspended' cultivation, which came from Spain, were adopted by a few French mussel farmers, but the most recent innovation, which is used along the Breton coast, is the method of raising mussels in channels or tributaries *entre deux eaux*, or just under the surface of the water.

The most prized mussels are the Breton Pertuis. The Mediterranean Bouzigues also have their fans. Mussels imported from Holland and Spain are larger but often shrink with cooking.

Mussels should be alive when you purchase them. It is wise to check the ticket attached to their packaging which attests to their health. Mussels must be eaten perfectly fresh and, of course, healthy. Reject any mussel that does not close itself tightly in response to the slightest pressure. If you must store them, take them out of their plastic bags as soon as possible, roll them in several damp cloths so that they will not open, and put them in the salad drawer of the refrigerator.

To prepare mussels, scrape the shells to remove all the debris stuck there. Remove the beard by pulling toward the rounded end of the shell.

*Here is the recipe for mussels so dear to my native region of Poitou.*

Wash them repeatedly in a large basin, brushing them vigorously to remove any sand they might be retaining. When they knock against each other, they will stay closed naturally, holding in all their delicious natural juices. Do not let mussels soak: if they open, they will lose some of their sea water and with it much of their flavour. They may be eaten raw, as oysters are, with a squeeze of lemon and a dash of vinegar, but they are more popular cooked.

The most classic way of cooking mussles is *à la marinière*, or in white wine sauce. In a large saucepan, pour white wine over chopped shallots. Add a few knobs of butter, a bouquet garni of parsley stalks, and a little ground pepper. Let these ingredients cook for 5 minutes, then add the mussels and some chopped parsley. Cover and cook, stirring from time to time. As soon as the mussels open, remove them from the heat.

To make the *mouclade* so dear to my native region of Poitou, drain the mussels *à la marinière*. Remove the larger half of the shell and arrange the mussels on a serving dish. Reduce the cooking juices in the pan, then add cream and a pinch of thyme. Cover the mussels lightly with the cream sauce, then glaze the mussels gently in the oven. Though some use an egg yolk for this, to me it seems unnecessary. However, I do like adding a julienne of mushrooms, leeks, fennel and a little curry powder.

A piece of advice: do not cook the mussels that float in the basin as you are washing them, since they have often lost their sea water and will only fill up on tap water and sink back to the bottom. Do not try to force open and eat a mussel that does not open in the course of cooking, since if the adductor muscle did not respond to the heat while cooking, the mussel was not good to begin with. Watch out for undercooked mussels! If you have doubts about the odour of any of them, discard them. No matter what recipe you follow, to appreciate mussels at their best, do not overcook them.

One spectacular approach typical of the Saintonge region is the *éclade*. This is a very old recipe in which the mussels are arranged, pointed end up, on a piece of wood that has already been soaked in water. The mussels are arranged very tightly against one another, in a circle so that they will not open and lose their water. Then they are covered with dry pine needles or, better, vine shoots which are then set aflame. As soon as the shells start to blacken, a piece of cardboard is used to fan them and blow away the cinders. Once cooked, the mussels are eaten hot, without fear of burning the fingers, with country bread and butter.

There are many ways to prepare mussels, all of them delicious: fried on skewers, grilled, stuffed, or in a salad, as in the following recipe.

## MUSSELS WITH CHIVES

SERVES 4

**4 lb (2 kg) of mussels, cooked**
*à la marinière*
**3 generous tablespoons**
**mayonnaise**
**1 generous tablespoon**
**chopped chives**

1. Take off the larger half of each mussel shell and place the mussels in a salad bowl.

2. Whisk a little of the juices from the *marinière* sauce with the mayonnaise until you have a velvety sauce.

3. Mix the sauce together with the mussels and chopped chives.

4. Keep the salad refrigerated.

*Serve cold*
*with a fresh and*
*lively white Muscadet*
*de Sèvre et Maine .*

# .LOBSTER.

This exceptional seafood is the pontiff of crustaceans. It belongs to the family of decapods, but note that it is not the husband of the crayfish! It can live for 50 years and attains an impressive size – up to 3 1/4 ft (1 m) in length and 44 lb (20 kg). The lobster has 10 claws, the first ambulatory pair equipped with large and powerful pincers which are a formidable weapon.

*Cardinal of the sea, pontiff of crustaceans, the lobster is exquisitely delicate.*

The body of the cardinal of the seas is protected by a shell impregnated with calcium obtained from the water, as well as sand. The lobster sheds the shell when it outgrows it. Mating occurs between a hard-shelled male and a female who has shed her shell less than 48 hours earlier. Should the lobster lose a limb, it will be regenerated with the next moulting.

The sedentary lobster takes refuge in the deep sea, preferring rocky cavities that hide good reserves of food. Even though it is a solitary creature, it is not rare to find it in the company of a conger eel: the lobster is waiting for the eel to lay eggs so that it may eat them! The conger eel, for its part, is always on the lookout for the moment when the lobster sheds its shell, when it will be vulnerable and easy prey. This is truly one of nature's vicious battles!

In general, the lobster is captured with the aid of traps baited with fresh or saltwater fish. The best is the dark blue European variety, which is found in zones up to 394 ft (120 m) deep from the north of Norway to the Mediterranean. The exquisitely succulent lobster from the coasts of Brittany's Finistère is renowned for its fine flesh and fragrance. Once abundant, it has become a great rarity.

The European lobster's American cousin is a little different – it is brownish-maroon in colour, and its thorax bulges more. Found along the northeast coast of the United States and Canada, it is caught with traps and trawls at depths of up to 1640 ft (500m). However, the American lobster's flavour is not as good, and it therefore costs about two times less than the European variety.

Between May and September is the best time to eat lobster, and it becomes more affordable – it is often half the price it commands during the end-of-the-year festivities! Avoid buying pre-cooked lobsters. In general, these animals died before cooking but have been cooked anyway so as not to be counted a loss. As soon as the lobster dies, its flesh becomes soft, and seeps away in the form of a viscous, transparent liquid. Lobsters must be bought alive and vigorous, with bright eyes and an agreeable odour. If the animal has spent too much time in transit or in a tank, it will have lost both its smell and its taste.

Choose a heavy lobster, preferably a female, as they have a finer flesh and flavour than the males. To identify the female, turn her over and look at the barred shell over her stomach: there is a hollow where the eggs are stored. On the male, this same area will bulge slightly. Discard any lobster that carries the eggs in her tail – it means she is old and her flesh will have lost its tenderness.

The first thing you should do is wash the lobster in running water to remove all impurities that might spoil its taste. It may be poached in a court-bouillon, steamed (which toughens the meat somewhat), grilled or roasted in the oven. Before roasting or grilling, blanch the lobster for 2 minutes in boiling salted water to kill it as fast as possible and preserve the tenderness of the flesh.

To grill lobster, first blanch it, then split it in half lengthwise. Lightly crack its claws. Season with salt and pepper. Mix together a pinch of curry powder, a little star anise, a clove of garlic, some basil and a little olive oil, then lightly brush this mixture over the lobster's flesh. Place it under the grill, being careful not to let it turn or tip while cooking so that all the juices will stay in the shell. If you are using a barbecue, never allow the flesh to come into contact with the fire, since it will dry up and lose all its juice.

Lobster may also be roasted in a very hot oven: allow 10 to 15 minutes for a 1 1/4–1 3/4 lb (500-800g) lobster. Keep it well basted with olive oil during cooking. As soon as the shell turns red, cover the lobster with a

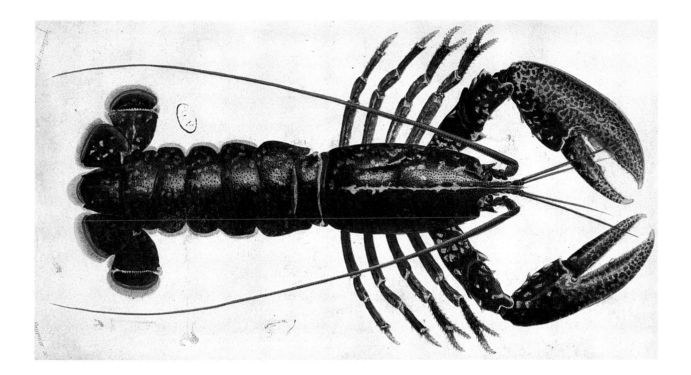

handful of seaweed and allow it to finish roasting. The perfume of iodine makes lobster sublime. Formerly, Breton fishermen cooked lobsters in wooden traps filled with seaweed. Once everything had burned, the lobster was done.

Lobster may also be served fried *à la meunière*. First blanch the lobster, then cut it into large pieces without removing the shell. Quickly fry it in a little butter and season it with a little salt and curry powder. If by chance you have a lobster that is in the process of moulting, cook it that way: it will be divine.

In my opinion, one of the best ways to cook lobster is *à la nage:* quickly poached in court-bouillon so that the flavour will not be too diluted. For this reason, I like using a pressure cooker, which permits me to cook while using a minimum of liquid.

All sorts of recipes for lobster exist, notably the traditional variation called *à l'américaine* or *à l'armoricaine* (in a tomato and shallot-based sauce), named for its reputedly Breton origin, though opinions differ on this. Two of my friends, the much-missed Alain Chapel (whose restaurant is in Mionnay dans l'Ain, near Lyon) and Jean Delaveyne (in Paris) are known for their remarkable lobster *île de Sein*, a ragout with potatoes, inspired by Breton tradition.

# LOBSTER WITH SAUTERNES

**SERVES 2**

**1 lobster, weighing about
1 3/4 lb (800g)**

**1 carrot**

**3 small young onions**

**2 3/4 oz (70g) butter**

**salt and ground pepper**

**1/2 pint (300ml) of Sauternes
(white wine)**

**3 1/2 fl oz (100ml) fresh
orange juice**

**thin slice of fresh ginger, cut
into julienne strips**

**5 sprigs of saffron**

**2 sprigs of parsley, finely
chopped**

1. Wash the lobster and blanch for 2 minutes in boiling salted water, then drain.

2. Finely slice the carrot and onions into rounds. Put them in a casserole with 1 1/4 oz (30g) of butter and a dash of salt. Cover and cook, without allowing the vegetables to brown.

3. In a pressure cooker, combine the carrot, onions, lobster, Sauternes, orange juice, julienned ginger, the remaining butter, saffron, and a pinch of salt and ground pepper.

4. Place the pressure cooker over a high heat. Cover, and count 4 minutes from the time you seal the pressure cooker. Shake the pressure cooker from time to time so that the ingredients do not stick to the pan. Once you remove the pressure cooker from the heat, let it stand for 3 minutes before removing the lid.

5. Remove the lobster and cut it in half lengthwise. Devein the tail and the creamy substance from the cranial cavity. Place the halved tail on a serving dish.

6. Bring the juices remaining in the pressure cooker back to a boil. Season and add the chopped parsley. Pour the sauce and vegetables over the lobster and serve.

*A Meursault Genevrières
makes a wonderful accompaniment.*

# .TUNA.

Among this marvellous fish of the high seas, the white *germon* is the king of all the varieties. By nature gregarious, tuna travel from the Azores, through the Gulf of Gascony and continue up to the north of Ireland, where they dive to greater depths before their return, which concludes the migratory cycle.

*Contrary to popular belief, the best part of the tuna is the belly.*

And what a majestically beautiful fish the tuna is, with its delicate sculpting! Tuna are most easily distinguished by their long pectoral fins, which join the second dorsal fin, a profile which permits them to manoeuvre rapidly and jump, even to lift themselves out of the water and fly – a feat familiar to rod and line fishermen, whose sport lends itself to moments of high drama. Once aboard the boat, tuna are immediately decapitated, gutted and cleaned. In France, germon fishing begins in June and the season lasts until September. Tuna are very much in demand. They are also capricious and highly influenced by the weather.

A true summer food, tuna may be imprinted with the magic of the sun and flavoursome accents from distant lands. Whether prepared in a fragrant farandole of onions, garlic, tomatoes, spices, courgettes, artichokes, carrots and potatoes or bathed in saffron and wild herbs, tuna is a tasty and healthy summer indulgence.

It is marvellous roasted in a large casserole, like veal, according to some gourmets. Tuna is also excellent cold, carved into fine escalopes and accompanied by its own lightly spiced juices. It is tastier still when accompanied by toast that has been rubbed with garlic – a wonderful medley of flavours.

There is one part of this noble fish that is very much appreciated by fishermen, yet remains little known to the general public: its underbelly. Certainly the best part, this is the treasure of this migratory fish. All tuna, and red tuna in particular,

are especially sought after by the Japanese, who eat it raw, and it is true that this part of the fish is incomparable.

Regardless of conventional wisdom, the best part of many long-bodied fish is the belly, and this part is much superior in gustatory subtlety than the back, where the muscles are long and taut. The belly of the *germon* is composed of innumerable short little muscles that support the abdomen. This is the origin of the famous little fillets that certain notable purveyors of tuna marinate in oil, but this product is relatively rare, since the belly of an entire tuna is necessary to fill one little tin of confit – a real gourmet delight.

One simple Breton preparation is whole belly of tuna *mitonée*, or simmered. First, put the fish in salt for a few days then soak it in clear water and cook it in the oven on a bed of potatoes and onions. Prepared with a thousand secrets bequeathed by a tradition of cooking tuna, this dish has a unique taste.

To make a piece of tuna more delicate, it must be trimmed a little, without removing its skin. Wash the fish well, sponge it off and dry it. Cover it with coarse sea salt, using 5 oz per lb (150g per 450 g), and a fragrant mix of thyme, bay leaves and black pepper. Cover both sides well, place it in a pan or casserole and keep it in the refrigerator for 2 or 3 days, depending on the size of the cut. Then take it out of the brine and wash it, leaving it in running water for a few seconds. Put the fish in a steamer and cook it for 15 minutes for every 2 lb (1 kg). This short preliminary cooking is the indispensable first step for many renowned chefs, and it also applies to other seafood such as sturgeon.

The popular mackerel in white wine is always treated with these preliminaries of salting and steaming before receiving its aromatic dressing. This is also the case for all tuna conserved in oil, as well as sardines packed in oil (lightly fried beforehand). Personally, I consider this to be an essential culinary tactic in the preparation of *germon*.

At sea, fishermen usually cut a few slices from the first *germon* captured of the day, spice it with garlic, cover it in oil, and expose it to sunlight for several hours. The next day, the slices are eaten raw with butter, lemon, and toast – a true summer delight.

While fishing one day, my friends Gwenn-Aël Bolloré (a specialist in marine biology and oceanography) and Jean Delaveyne (the illustrious chef known for his love of seafood) decided to conduct an experiment. As much for curiosity as to the habits of seafaring men, they examined the stomachs of the tuna they caught in order to determine an inventory of its diet. They found that the stomach of the *germon* resembles a large spongy morel to such a degree that they decided to whip up a *fricassée* of tuna stomach (as one would with eel or lamprey) with wine, leeks, onions, bacon, mushrooms and garlic croutons. The result was a magnificent dish, which illustrates why the fish has been christened 'the Sea Morel'.

Aside from the many renowned classic recipes for tuna, the *omelette du curé*, with or without carp milt but with pieces of tuna, is a unique and authentic French masterpiece which is quick and simple to make.

# TUNA OMELETTE

SERVES 2

**1 small shallot, chopped**

**3 oz (75g) butter**

**salt and ground pepper**

**6 eggs**

**chopped chives and parsley**

**2 oz (50g) tuna in oil**

1. Place the chopped shallot and 1/2 oz (15 g) of butter in a frying pan and let the shallot sweat without browning.

2. Put a pinch of salt and ground pepper in a bowl, then break the eggs into the bowl.

3. Add the chopped chives and parsley.

4. Beat the eggs until they are just mixed. Incorporate the tuna and the cooked chopped shallots.

5. In a clean frying pan, heat approximately 2 oz (50g) of butter.

6. Pour the eggs into the pan. Using a spatula, bring the parts that start to stick to the sides of the pan into the centre. Continue until the omelette has reached the desired consistency: liquid, medium or well done.

7. Depending on the consistency you prefer, leave the pan on the heat for a few seconds without stirring the eggs.

8. Fold the omelette and place it on a preheated plate.

9. Spread the rest of the butter over the surface of the omelette so that it shines.

*Serve with*
*a vibrant and aromatic white*
*Côtes du Roussillon.*

# .TOMATOES.

The star of the summer, this lovely rubicund, curvaceous fruit exudes charm. The fragrance of pleasingly plump tomato is seduction itself.

Originally from the American tropics, the tomato was imported by the Conquistadors in the 16th century. For a long time, it was nothing more to the gourmet than a simple vegetable from the South. In northern France, the tomato was cultivated solely for ornamentation, since it was considered to be a poisonous plant. During the Revolution, tomatoes were brought from Marseille to Paris, after which they established their good name – after all, the colour red ruled the day at the time.

Now consumed year-round, tomatoes are the tastiest during the summer months, when they are gorged with sunlight. In France, the tomato is the most popularly cultivated produce, even more than the potato, and it is widely appreciated for its fresh aroma as well as its vitamins.

While tomatoes are generally red, there are also yellow, purplish, and even white varieties, though their interest is purely decorative. There are three types of

*Summer's lovely, seductive and pleasingly plump fruit: the tomato.*

tomato: round (including the diminutive cherry tomato), elongated, and ribbed and flattened.

Tomatoes should be firm to the touch but juicy, with a brilliant smooth skin and uniform colour. Avoid any with spots, traces of fading, splits or bruises which are the result of rough handling. Tomatoes that are a little green will ripen easily when kept in a warm place. Every part of the tomato is edible, though the skin contains substances that are irritating to the stomach. Many recipes recommend removing them. To do so, take a small knife, cut a cone around the stem and pull it out, along with part of the core. Put the tomato in boiling water for 15 seconds, cool rapidly under running water, dry and skin.

Though the above is the traditional approach for skinning tomatoes, I prefer a quicker method by which the tomato does not absorb water: once the stem has been pulled out, spear the tomato with a fork, hold it over a flame and turn it until the skin blisters. Do not heat it for long, or the tomato will cook. The skin should peel off with no problem. Then quarter the tomato and remove the seeds and the pulp until only the flesh remains.

The tomato plays an important role in the kitchen, since few vegetables lend themselves so well to such a variety of uses. Its lightly acidic, sugary flavour marries well with all sorts of seafood, fish, meat, vegetables, eggs, pasta, etc. It is also a staple for excellent hot or cold soups and even preserves and very refreshing sorbets. Tomatoes are simultaneously a condiment, vegetable and fruit.

Considering how prized the tomato is today, who would guess that its role in the kitchen is a relatively recent development? Celebrated chef Adolphe Dugléré, who was then at Trois Frères Provençaux in Paris, was the first to serve it at its best, notably in a recipe for fish: skin the tomatoes and remove the seeds and the pulp, leaving only the tender flesh. Dice them, place them on a generously buttered porcelain dish and sprinkle them with finely chopped onions . Arrange the fish on top and add a little dry white wine for bouquet

(if you have none, add water); the liquid should not cover the fish. Season with a little bouquet garni, salt and ground pepper. Cover the pan with aluminium foil, and put it in the oven at 425°F/220°C/Gas Mark 7. Cook the fish gently and remove it from the platter, putting it aside momentarily, but keeping it warm. Pour its juice into a saucepan and reduce over a medium heat until lightly syrupy. Add a few knobs of fresh butter and prepare the sauce as you would a *beurre blanc*. Taste and correct the seasoning if necessary, adding a squeeze of lemon and a sprinkle of parsley. Blanket the fish in the sauce, which has been dubbed *Dugléré* sauce.

The most traditional way to handle tomatoes is to stuff them. There are innumerable variations for adapting the tomato to any palate or circumstance. Enrich your recipes by throwing in almost anything that crosses your imagination: vegetables, meats, rice . . .

When combined with courgettes, aubergines and bell peppers, the tomato constitutes an excellent base for one of the famous dishes from the south of France: ratatouille, another specialty of the season – and it is true that the sunny aromas of basil, thyme, olive and garlic go so well with the summer!

*Codfish à la Dugléré*

# HOT MUSSELS WITH COLD TOMATOES

**All the gustatory pleasure in this recipe comes from the contrast between hot and cold.**

SERVES 4

2–2 1/2 lb (1–1.2 kg) Bouchot mussels
a knob of fresh butter
3 1/2 fl oz (100 ml) dry white wine
1 small onion, chopped
salt and ground pepper
11 oz (300 g) ripe tomatoes
2 fl oz (50 ml) olive oil
2 leaves of basil, chopped
pinch of curry powder, wine vinegar

1. Clean the mussels. In a saucepan, combine the butter, white wine and chopped onion. Bring the mixture to a boil, season it with pepper and add the mussels. Stir often, removing them as soon as they are half-open. Shell them.

2. Wash and skin the tomatoes. Using a fine blade, put them through the food processor and then strain them. Season the tomato sauce with salt and pepper. Add a little curry powder and the chopped basil and place the sauce in the refrigerator.

3. When you are ready to serve, heat the olive oil in a saucepan, quickly seal the mussels and remove them as soon as they are hot.

4. Pour the well-chilled sauce onto the dinner plates and cover it with the cooked mussels.

5. Dip the tines of a fork in vinegar and sprinkle the mussels with a few droplets.

*Serve immediately
with a chilled white wine
from Cassis.*

# .SALT.

Salt, the indispensable condiment to good cooking, has been a precious commodity since the days of antiquity. A precious gift of nature appreciated all around the world, salt ranks with three other major elements of nourishment: olive oil, bread and wine.

Salt is a sacred element; it even appears as a liturgical ingredient. In the Christian religion, it is used in baptismal ceremonies to symbolize purity, wisdom, and power – it permits ascension to the 'light' of faith. It holds a privileged place in the practice of exorcism, and makes evil forces flee. It is also the symbol of friendship and hospitality – oriental tradition dictates the sharing of bread and salt to signify an alliance that may not be broken. Nothing can replace salt, and it never goes stale. Since the beginning of history, salt has been a source of commerce. Legionnaires in the Roman Empire were paid in salt, or 'sal', which is the origin of the word 'salary'. Many countries had a tax on salt. In France, the duty on salt, called *la gabelle*, was instituted in the 14th century. This was a very unpopular move since not only was salt taxed but each year the populace was obliged to buy a certain quantity of it from the king's storehouse at a fixed price, regardless of how much would actually be consumed. After a long and tumultuous period, the *gabelle* was lifted in 1790; however, tax on salt was not completely

*The crystalline* **fleur** *de sel, which is gathered at sea level, remains one of the world's marvels.*

abolished by the National Assembly until 1945!

In France, only one thing concerning salt remains forbidden: to draw even one litre of salt from sea water without the authorization of the Minister of Finance. These days, alimentary salt is still the object of taxation and of production and distribution monopolies in certain countries.

For thousands of years, man has mined this white gold using the same fundamental principles. Salt is found in the sea, of course, and in the earth, in the salt deposits left by seas that have long since evaporated. It is mined either in the solid mineral state, or in brine – saturation by the addition of fresh water, or by filtration. Sea salt, which is appreciated both for its natural origin and its distinctive flavour, is harvested in salt marshes. After being conducted a little at a time into artificial evaporation basins, the sea water begins its long journey. During the summer the water evaporates, leaving salt deposits, and this fruit of the sea, sun, and wind is harvested. The *fleur de sel* (greyish salt from the top of the beds) is one of the world's marvels. Salt from the Bay of Guérande in Brittany is highly prized for its incomparable flavour and its delicate violet fragrance.

All over the world, salt has always played a double role of seasoning and preservation. Upon the discovery of the New World, it contributed to the development of salted cod and was, until the 19th century, the only means of long preservation. Its essential function became to season food, to bring out and enhance flavours and to whet the appetite. Salt's role in relation to the human body is of primary importance, since it regulates hydration.

Salt exists in many forms. Coarse salt, whether grey or refined, is more highly regarded than crystallized salt, followed by table salt, which is even more refined. The use of different types of salt requires some judgement. Personally, when I make *pommes frites*, I always mix fine salt, which salts deeply, with *fleur de sel*, which crunches a bit between the teeth – delicious.

It is important always to add salt at the right time. For a roast, add salt when you begin to cook it, and again when you take it from the oven: the salt is absorbed into the meat and helps it relax before it is eaten. To obtain golden-brown sautéed potatoes that do not stick together, add salt only when they are cooked. To preserve the green tint of vegetables, blanch them or cook them in heavily salted water. Allow 1/2 oz (15g) of salt for every 1 3/4 pt (1 litre) of water, and only salt the water as it begins to boil. It is also at this precise moment that you must add the vegetables. The action of the salt preserves the chlorophyll, which gives vegetables a lively colour and keeps them pleasing to the eye. In addition to the common uses of salt, cooking in a crust of salt is one of the most spectacular and exquisite yet simple methods to cook fish and keep all the original flavour without salting it in the least.

# SEA BREAM IN A SALT CRUST

SERVES 4

**1 sea bream, approx 3 lb (1.5 kg)**
**4 – 6 lb (2–3kg) coarse sea salt**
**1 sprig of fresh thyme**
**freshly ground pepper**
**olive oil**

1. Preheat the oven to 475°F/240°C, Gas Mark 9.

2. Clean the fish, cut off its fins and remove its gills. Do not scale it. Rinse it quickly under running water.

3. Sprinkle pepper on the belly of the fish and garnish it with fresh thyme.

4. In a casserole, spread a layer of salt about 3/4 inch (2 cm) thick. Place the fish on top, and then cover it generously with salt – it should be completely buried. Sprinkle the top with a few drops of water.

5. Place the casserole in the oven and let the fish cook for about 45 minutes.

6. Remove the casserole from the oven and chip off the salt crust. Remove the skin and place the fillets on warm plates.

7. Sprinkle the fillets with pepper and drizzle a little olive oil over them.

*Enjoy this succulent meal*
*with a richly aromatic white wine*
*from Burgundy, such as a*
*Chassagne-Montrachet.*

# .OLIVE OIL.

Olive oil is divine and sacred. The Latin language confirms it: the olive tree and its fruit are both called olea, which is the root of oleum, or oil. It is the oil of our ancestors, whether the roots be Mediterranean, Hebrews, pagans, Arabs, Greeks or Latin.

I love olive oil, that marvellous product that completes the triad with bread and wine. It is the soul of cuisine which, like butter, finds an expression in and of itself in the kitchen. For thousands of years, it has figured in our nourishment. It is the oil of our memories and celebrations. It is an integral part of our research, as our cuisine improves and becomes more refined. It is close to everything that is natural on the earth and is part of nature's plan which has created all things so that we may be happy at table.

All the ancient peoples of the Mediterranean lay claim to the discovery and cultivation of the olive tree. Originally of Asian origin, the olive tree was, according to some historians, planted in Greece by Hercules, whose head was wreathed with its branches as he returned from his glorious adventures in foreign lands. An olive tree is said to have been planted on Mount Olympus, hence its origin as the symbol of victory. According to other sources, it was brought back from Egypt to Athens by Cecrops. The Greeks had such a veneration for the tree that they made it the symbol of wisdom, abundance, peace, power and even of purification and the sacred. In Genesis, the dove released by Noah at the end of the flood came back to the ark with an olive branch in its beak, in witness to the appeasement of Divine wrath. Jesus prayed and meditated his Passion in the olive gardens. It is oil which was used to anoint the priests and kings of Israel, from which evolved the name of the Messiah in Hebrew and Christ in Greek. These words signify 'holy oil' and 'the Lord's anointed'. Much later, the kings of France were consecrated with the same oil and today it is used for extreme unction.

The olive tree and its fruit are an intrinsic part of the history of humanity. How can we not be fascinated by this tree which is tormented with a suffering born of an ancient history? It suffers the unending challenge

*Olive oil joins bread and wine as the third element of the culinary triad.*

to better yield its little fruits, which bloom on branches whose leaves are so delicate that they turn silver at the slightest breeze. This age-old tree belongs to the family of evergreens, and is extremely hardy – it may live as long as 300 or 400 years. It flowers at the end of spring when, for about eight days, the buds unfold in all their glory. For every 20 flowers that bloom, one olive will emerge, on average. The stone becomes harder in the course of the summer, and the flesh becomes plump. The end of September is harvest time for the earlier varieties, while late olives are harvested at the end of February. Another characteristic that makes this plant so endearing is that the harvesting of olives traditionally must be done by hand.

Once sorted, and sometimes washed by hand, olives are crushed and kneaded before being pressed in order to extract their liquid. This thick black juice is later filtered, centrifuged, then decanted so as to isolate the oil from the water the olive contained. This is called the first pressing, and entails absolutely no chemical intervention. Virgin olive oil is the queen of cuisine – an extraordinary nectar which has vintages in the same manner as fine wine. The individual terrain plays a predominant role in the oil's flavour and the choice is vast. Explore and savour this veritable treasure of nature – whether thick or fluid, of a clear amber, golden yellow or almost green colour, with a soft or almost fruity flavour, there is always an olive oil that will seduce the most discriminating of palates.

All oils have one thing in common: they are marvellous carriers of fragrance. Olive oil, however, is the one that best lends itself to osmosis. Put a pinch of saffron pistil or curry powder in olive oil and it will take on that flavour. Add a little basil and it will be perfectly seasoned for pasta. Spray grilled shellfish with a little olive oil mixed with curry powder, a little star anise, a clove of garlic and some basil. I recommend having different varieties of olive oil on hand: curry, saffron, red pepper, basil, tarragon, etc. Pay careful attention to its storage, since olive oil becomes rancid in sunlight and oxydizes in contact with air. Look for opaque bottles and never forget to replace the bottle top right away. Aromatic olive oils will always bring their inimitable flavours to salads, vegetables, meat and fish and so on.

Olive oil resists heat better than other types of oil. It can be used for sautéing and frying. Marinating in olive oil is a way to preserve not only fish but also cheese: arrange small pieces of goat cheese in a short-necked jar. Cover them with olive oil, add a few grains of green pepper and juniper berry, thyme and bay laurel. Stopper the bottle and let it sit in a cool place before indulging yourself.

Olive oil is also an essential base for sauces, mayonnaise and garlic mayonnaise, and as a seasoning of salads and main courses. Sprinkle a little olive oil, salt from Guérande, pepper and a little lemon on a fish, then steam it, cook it in a papillote or grill it – the result will be superb. You will have the same success with raw mushrooms, preferably ceps, sprinkled with fresh walnuts, or with fillets of raw beef, sliced very thinly – an Italian speciality (Venetian in particular) which is called carpaccio.

Thanks to olive oil, the most banal of foods take on sunny accents, and the most refined of dishes become radiant with fragrance.

# FILLETS OF MULLET
## IN OLIVE OIL

**SERVES 4**

**4 fillets of red mullet, about**

**6 oz (175g) each**

**7 fl oz (200 ml) extra virgin**

**olive oil**

**1 shallot, chopped**

**1/2 onion, finely chopped**

**bouquet garni**

**salt and ground pepper**

**1 sprig of basil**

**a knob of butter**

**1 tomato, skinned, seeded**

**and diced**

**1/2 lemon**

1. Scale the fillets of mullet (or have the fishmonger scale them for you).

2. Put 2 tablespoons of olive oil in a saucepan and add the chopped shallots and onion. Let them sweat without browning and add the mullet head and bones, cut into large pieces. Stir for 2 or 3 minutes then add the bouquet garni. Cover the mixture with water, add a pinch of salt and bring it to a boil. Let it cook for about 5 minutes, then run the sauce through a fine sieve.

3. Reduce the sauce to about 2 fl oz (50 ml), then add 1/3 oz (10g) of basil leaves which have been crumpled in your hand. Cover the saucepan and let it steep for 5 minutes, then strain.

4. Return the infusion to the heat and incorporate 3 1/2 fl oz (100 ml) of olive oil, whisking briskly as you would for a *beurre blanc*. Finish by incorporating a knob of butter, then add salt and pepper. Add the tomato, a tablespoon of chopped basil if necessary, and the lemon juice.

5. Heat two non-stick frying pans, pour 1 tablespoon of olive oil into each, and place the fillets in the pan, skin down. Season and cook for 30 seconds. Turn them and season the other side, then remove them from the pan.

6. Pour the warm sauce onto warm plates, then arrange the fillets on top and serve immediately.

***Serve with***

***a subtle and slightly acidic***

***white Hermitage.***

# .AUBERGINES.

The aubergine is a summer vegetable par excellence, and its qualities are best enjoyed during the height of the season. Originally from India, this beautiful vegetable was cultivated in China before the Middle Ages and, thanks to the Arabs, was finally brought to Western Europe. Aubergines come from the same family as the tomato, and shared its unfortunate reputation of being poisonous. It was not until the closing years of the 18th century, that this ornamental vegetable was recognized and appreciated for its culinary virtues.

Whether it is round or oblong, Episcopal mauve, deep violet, black or even white, every type of aubergine is delicious. When buying them, make sure they are fresh and not overripe, since the formation of seeds diminishes the quality of the flesh. The smaller ones are firmer and delicately chubby, with a softer flesh and fewer seeds. The skin should be tight and smooth, polished and glossy, without any spots.

It is impossible to separate aubergines from the traditional Mediterranean way of savouring them, because they are most frequently associated with tomatoes and olive oil. Here is a style of cuisine that smells as good as a holiday! Aubergines may be enjoyed puréed, in a quiche, a gratin or in fritters, stuffed, fried . . . I find fried aubergines an excellent accompaniment for red meat, particularly sirloin.

To fry an aubergine, first peel it, then cut it into slices of about 1/4 inch (6mm) thick. Coat both sides of a slice with flour, then dip it in a beaten whole egg that has been seasoned with salt and pepper and coat it with sieved breadcrumbs. Fry the slices in olive oil or groundnut oil, either in a frying pan or a deep-fryer if you have one. They should be golden brown and crunchy.

You could also try a caviar of aubergines, a sort of 'poor man's caviar'. Cook the whole unpeeled aubergine in the oven for a good hour, basted with olive oil, then halve it and scoop out the flesh. Finely chop an onion and put it in a drizzle of olive oil over a medium heat to glaze it. Purée garlic and basil leaves, then combine with the aubergine with the onion confit and mix the ingre-

*Take advantage of the summer to cook up a succulent ratatouille.*

dients together well. Season with salt, pepper, and a pinch of ground nutmeg. Next, drizzle olive oil into the mixture a little at a time, as if you were making a mayonnaise, and stir constantly with a whisk or use a blender. Aubergine caviar should be served on toast, and makes a good garnish for fish, meat, or any other dish, hot or cold. You may also wish to add a few pounded anchovy fillets or a purée of bell peppers, black olives or tomatoes . . .

It was once common to peel aubergines. Today, this practice is practically abandoned, except in a few instances. Aubergines may also be drained, especially if they are large, by covering them in salt for a while to eliminate bitterness. They must then be rinsed well before they are cooked. Prepared this way, aubergines absorb less oil during cooking. Though refined palates may scorn the idea, try aubergines with ceps, which have a similarly pronounced taste.

Take advantage of this beautiful season, when all sun-drenched vegetables are at their best, to cook up a succulent ratatouille.

# RATATOUILLE

1. Skin the tomatoes, halve them and remove the seeds. Drain them to remove the juices, which you set aside. Dice the flesh and set that aside also.

2. In a saucepan, combine the cold olive oil and the onions with a pinch of salt. Cover and cook until translucent – do not allow them to brown. Then add the minced peppers and a pinch of salt. Cover and cook over a low heat for 4 to 5 minutes.

3. Next, add the tomatoes. Stir the ingredients well, then allow them to cook for another 4 to 5 minutes without browning. Add a pinch of salt.

4. Pour the tomato juice into the saucepan and add the bouquet garni, chopped garlic and a little pepper. Cover the pan and simmer over a low heat for about 30 minutes, by which time all the vegetables should be done.

5. In the meantime, pour about 1/4 inch (6 mm) of olive oil into a large frying pan. Heat, and add the julienned courgettes. Do not use salt, or the courgettes

---

**SERVES 8**

**2 lb (1 kg) tomatoes**

**1/2 pint (300 ml) olive oil**

**2 medium-sized onions, minced**

**salt and pepper**

**1 red pepper and 1 green pepper, skinned and minced**

**1 bouquet garni**

**4 cloves garlic, peeled and finely chopped**

**3 small courgettes, washed and julienned**

**2 small aubergines, washed and julienned**

**pinch of fresh thyme**

**pinch of saffron (optional)**

---

will exude their juices. Once they are gently browned, remove the courgettes from the heat, drain off the excess oil, and set them aside.

6. In the same frying pan, heat the remaining olive oil. Add the aubergines. Brown and drain them as you did the courgettes.

7. Combine the courgettes and aubergines. Sprinkle them with salt, pepper and a pinch of fresh thyme. Then add them to the stewed onions, peppers and tomatoes. If you like, you may add a pinch of saffron. Cover the pan and let it simmer over a low heat for 30 minutes.

*Serve ratatouille*
*hot or cold, alone*
*or as a garnish for shellfish,*
*fish or meat, accompanied*
*by a chilled rosé such as*
*Côtes de Provence.*

# .MELON.

Of all the fruits in the kitchen garden, none is so much the object of gourmet desire as the melon. What could be more delicate, more profoundly fragrant than this king of the Cucurbitaceae?

The origins of the melon are not known but its cultivation is ancient, dating back to the beginning of the Christian era. Melons were introduced in France toward the end of the 15th century, when Charles VIII returned from his expedition to Italy. The cantaloupe gained its name because it was grown at Cantalupo, which was the popes' summer residence on the outskirts of Rome. Melons are produced by an annual vine of which there are numerous varieties, and they are classified into four groups:

• The globular cantaloupe, with a tough, ribbed, often warty rind. Its orange-red flesh is very fragrant. The cantaloupe, and most notably the Charentais variety, accounts for the greater part of French melon production.

• The *Sucrin* is an ovoid melon with a thick rind and fine, sweet orange flesh

• The *Brode* has different forms. Its surface is covered with a relief of sinuous grey lines, rather like an embroidery. Its flesh may vary from green to reddish-orange, and it is often less fragrant than other varieties.

• The winter melon, which matures belatedly, may have either a smooth or rough rind. It is harvested in the south of France and in countries of a warmer climate, such as Spain.

Melon production begins in mid April, sometimes earlier for those that are grown in greenhouses. The best season is from mid June to the end of August. At the end of October the harvest is over.

When choosing melons, inspect them carefully and choose healthy ones, without spots, bruises or traces of insect infestation. Regulations require that the stem be cut about 1 1/4 inches

*As a dessert or an hors d'oeuvre, treat yourself to melon, the king of the Cucurbitaceae.*

(3cm) from the fruit. A good melon is heavy for its size – if light, it is hollow, lacking juice. Look at the colour – it should be neither too green, nor too yellow. A green melon has not matured enough, or else does not contain enough sugar and will have little fragrance. The underside, opposite the stem, should be flexible when you press it with your thumb. The stem will be easy to detach. Odour is a sure guide. A ripe melon will have an agreeable, pervasive aroma, without smelling of ether, which is a sign of over-ripeness. At the other end from the stem there is an areola of variable size called an umbilicus. This pistillary scar is sometimes very developed and pigmented. It corresponds to variable and poor light conditions after flowering and does not at all indicate the sex of the melon!

Melons may be kept for four or five days in a cool airy place. Do not keep them in the refrigerator, since the odour will taint the other food there. If the skin is lightly split, eat the melon without delay.

Melon is most often eaten as an hors d'oeuvre. Eat it fresh, not chilled. It may be garnished with Banyuls (a sweet wine from Rouissillon in the south of France), port, a Charentes pineau (liqueur), or even a raspberry sauce. Purists prefer to serve it plain, with a glass of sweet wine.

Finely sliced Parma ham is, in my opinion, the ideal accompaniment for melon. Alternatively, it may be sprinkled with salt and ground pepper, for a mixture of spice and sugar which never ceases to stupefy foreigners, who regard this as heresy. It may also be cooked in chicken stock with fragrant mushrooms and ham for a traditional soup particularly favoured by the Chinese.

Sprinkled with a fine coating of sugar, melon makes a wonderful dessert. Some prefer it in a compote or a tart, or served chilled with other fruits. In sorbet, as presented in this recipe, melon is also a delight.

# MELON SORBET
# WITH BANYULS SAUCE

**SERVES 8**

**2 lb (1kg) ripe cantaloupe melon**

**juice of 2 lemons**

**75 oz (210g) sugar**

FOR THE SAUCE

**18 fl oz (500 ml) Banyuls**

**1/2 oz (15g) cornflour**

**1 1/4 oz (30g) sugar**

1. Quarter the melon and remove the seeds and rind. Weigh 1 3/4 lb (800g) of flesh and cut it into pieces.

2. Mix the melon with the lemon juice and sugar, then sieve.

3. Pour the ingredients into the ice-cream maker and turn it on.

4. Bring the Banyuls to a boil, flambé it and reduce it to about 14 fl oz (400 ml) .

5. Blend the cornflour with 2 or 3 tablespoons of water, then add it to the saucepan.

6. When it boils, take the sauce off the heat. Strain and chill.

*Serve the melon sorbet*
*with the chilled sauce along with a glass of rich*
*and subtle well-aged Banyuls.*

# .GRAPES.

September (or Fructidor in the Julian calendar, from 'Fructus', meaning fruit) is the month of golden-flavoured fruit. This is the time to delight in the regal grape, the food of Bacchus.

We owe our knowledge of cultivating this glorious fruit of the vine to the Hebrews, who first reaped its benefits. The Greeks and the Romans made wine from grapes, and the Mediterranean peoples knew how to dry this noble fruit; the most prized raisins still come from Corinth, Malaga and Smyrna. In France, the Gauls favoured viticulture. The monks, who needed wine for mass, improved the methods of wine production. From the earliest times, grapes have served to make wine, but they were also enjoyed at table, dried or fresh. Those vines which produce the best wine, such as Cabernet-Sauvignon or Chardonnay, are not necessarily delicious when eaten in their natural state.

There are many types of grape. Varieties which are destined to be pressed and bottled into wine offer tight bunches of juicy grapes which are necessary to obtain 'must' of good quality, while table grapes come in pretty, loose bunches – handfuls of delicious flavours.

The cultivation of grapes destined for the table dates from the great crisis of the end of the 19th century, when the eruption of phylloxera – a rapacious aphid – caused growers to develop new variations. The two oldest varieties of the French table grape are the Chasselas of Fontainebleau (long recognized as the best) and those from Moissac. For the gourmet, summer's end is the high season to appreciate clusters of sun-gorged grapes, whether white or red, round or oval, even if importation from warmer climates make it possible to enjoy them year round.

Choose grapes that are at the peak of maturity. Once harvested, they will ripen no further. If grapes

*September is the time to delight in the regal grape, the food of Bacchus.*

are overripe, they are easily detached from the stalk and must be eaten quickly. Grapes should be healthy, firm, of equal size, as uniform a colour as possible, regularly spaced on the bunch, preferably covered with a bloom which is an assurance of freshness. The stem should be supple and green. Buy grapes in small quantities, since it is a fragile fruit which does not store well. If you do store them, put them in a bowl covered with clingfilm in the refrigerator, and be sure to take the grapes out of the refrigerator well before they are to be eaten – the cold mutes their flavour. Always wash grapes in water with a dash of lemon before serving.

Grapes may be used in a number of preparations, both sweet and savoury. In the kitchen, grapes complement poultry, game, offal such as calves' liver and, most of all, foie gras. I recommend this delicious recipe to accompany pheasant, partridge and quail. Peel large muscat grapes and remove the seeds. Let them marinate in marc for 30 minutes. With a fork, delicately roll each grape in a mixture of flour, a lightly beaten egg, and sieved bread crumbs. Quickly dunk the grapes in a deep-fryer, removing them as soon as they are golden brown, and serve.

During the season, consider replacing the wine called for in fish sauces with fresh grape juice. Choose a grape that is not too sweet – its flavour will be more agreeable with the fish. Even better than fresh grape juice is verjuice, which comes from the little grapes cut from the vines after the harvest. Since they have been deprived of the sunlight they will never mature, and the vintners are kind enough to furnish me with them. I like to use verjuice to prepare herring roe. Even though this dish is no longer on my menu, people are still asking me for it!

Grape seeds may also be pressed to extract their oil, which I prefer to use when making mayonnaise, since it does not coagulate when stored in the refrigerator. As for desserts, the grape is a felicitous ingredient in fruit salad, tarts, sweets and preserves, and is wonderful in a sorbet.

## GRAPE SORBET WITH SAUCE

SERVES 8

**5 lb (2.5 kg) black grapes**

**3 1/4oz (80g) icing sugar**

**juice of 2 lemons**

1. Crush the grapes in a bowl and leave them to macerate overnight in the refrigerator.

2. Pass the crushed grapes through a sieve. Mix 1 3/4 pt (1 litre) of grape juice with the icing sugar and lemon juice. Put in the ice-cream maker for a velvety sorbet.

3. Reduce the remaining grape juice over the heat, skimming the surface as necessary, until you have a light syrup. Strain.

4. Pour the sauce into bowls and carefully top it with the sorbet.

*Serve with a full and*
*fragrant white Bonnezeaux*
*from the Loire.*

# .APPLES.

Whether crunchy, slightly acidic or sweet, all apples are delicious. This symbol of temptation goes back to the dawn of civilization, and was first crossbred and harvested by the Romans.

The apple tree is part of the Rosaceae family. Its seedlings do not grow true, and therefore its principal mode of reproduction is by grafting. Otherwise, it will be just the same wild apple tree it was originally. The blossom of most types of apple needs the pollen of another variety of apple tree to fertilize it. To this end, wind is an invaluable assistant and the bee is even more so. It is best to have many different varieties of apple tree in a single orchard; they produce more fruit than they would were they grown separately.

With so many varieties of apple, there is one to satisfy all tastes. They are classed in three categories: flat, which are squat with a large circumference; spheroid, which are more evenly round; and elongated, which are taller than they are round. The cider apple is different from the baking and table apples.

For all practical purposes, apples are available year round, but it is in autumn that they make the best table fruit. Choose them firm and shiny, free of wrinkles and bruises. To gauge their maturity, give the base a little flick with your finger. If you hear a dull thud, the apple is ripe. Always wash apples, since agrichemical products are used in their cultivation.

This fruit plays an important part in desserts. Do not confuse apple compote with apple conserve. To make a compote, quarter the apples, peel them, remove the pips and sprinkle the apples with lemon juice. Then plunge them into a simmering syrup flavoured with cinnamon and vanilla. Poach the apple quarters, then remove them from the syrup and allow them to cool. Gently reduce the syrup, then cover the apple quarters with the sauce and serve either unaccompanied or with ice cream. Apple conserve, on the other hand, is made by cooking apples with sugar and then reducing them to a purée.

*Enjoy apples warm and golden, with a splash of calvados.*

The apple tart in all its forms is the most popular dish in the world. The famous French *tarte Tatin* is the most well-known of all – its particular characteristic is that the dough is cooked on top and the apples caramelize in butter underneath. The tart is then flipped over and presented with the fruit on top. It is this dessert that made the reputation of the Tatin sisters, who had a hotel-restaurant in Lamotte-Beuvron, in the Loir-et-Cher, a century ago. This recipe comes from a very old tradition, since the tart has been cooked upside down in Orléans for centuries. Another easy-to-make traditional recipe is the apple *bonne femme*, a preparation in which the apple is infused with delicate flavours and retains its seductive appearance. Moreover, if there is only one at table, this dessert may be made with just a single apple. Core the apple, taking care to remove all the pips. With the point of a small knife, make little incisions all around and in the apple. Split a vanilla pod in two lengthwise and cut it into six strips. With a skewer, pierce the apple in six different, well-spaced places and insert the strips of vanilla into the holes. Place the apple in a buttered ovenproof dish and fill the centre of the apple with brown sugar and a generous knob of butter. Bake in the oven at a low heat. When the apple is nearly done, pour a little calvados or rum over the top. Enjoy it while it is still hot, golden and fragrant, with a little cream.

The uses of apples in patisserie are many and varied, since this fruit goes perfectly with cinnamon, vanilla, brown sugar, lemon, cream, raisins, calvados, rum . . .

Apples also figure in a wide variety of savoury dishes and salads, and are a particularly good complement to ham. Braised in butter, apples are the ideal accompaniment for blood pudding, duck and game. To prepare, peel an apple, cut it into quarters and remove the pips. Shape each quarter into an oval and roll it in fresh lemon juice so that it will not darken. Heat clarified butter in a frying pan over a high heat and add the apples. Once they have browned slightly, reduce the heat and finish cooking gently, turning them frequently. When the apples are done, strain them and pour a few drops of calvados over each piece. Served this way, they are the very essence of sweet temptation.

# APPLE UPSIDE-DOWN CAKE

SERVES 8

**5 Pippin apples**

**11 oz (300g) caster sugar**

**pinch of powdered cinnamon**

**5 1/4 oz (160g) butter**

**2 oz (50g) slivered almonds**

**3 eggs**

**3 1/2 oz (90g) crème fraîche**

**5 1/4 oz (160g) flour**

**2 oz (50g) raisins**

**2 fl oz (50 ml) calvados**

**8 fl oz (250 ml) vanilla**

**crème anglaise (optional)**

1. Peel the apples, quarter them, and remove the pips.

2. Arrange the apple slices in a pie dish and powder them with 2 oz (50g) of caster sugar and cinnamon. Dot them with 3 1/4 oz (80g) of butter and bake them in the oven, turning them often.

3. Butter the bottom and sides of a manqué mould and sprinkle it with slivered almonds.

4. Arrange the baked apples in the mould.

5. In the food processor, combine the eggs and 7 oz (200g) of caster sugar. Add 3 1/2 oz (90 g) of crème fraîche and 2 1/4 oz (60 g) of melted butter. Incorporate the flour and raisins, then pour the batter into the cake mould, covering the apples.

6. Bake in the oven at 350°F/180°C/Gas Mark 4 for about 25 minutes.

7. In the meantime, make a syrup with 2 oz (50g) of sugar and 3 tablespoons of water. Bring it to a boil, remove it from the heat and add the calvados.

8. Take the cake out of the oven and transfer it from the mould onto a plate. Glaze the top with syrup.

*Serve the cake warm,*
*with or without vanilla crème anglaise,*
*accompanied by a chilled,*
*velvety Sauternes.*

# .SHORTCRUST PASTRY.

The tart is one of the most popular dishes at French tables, and it is found in all the cuisines of the world. Many childhood memories are linked with this dessert of true epicurean delight. Adorned with seasonal fruits, the tart seems to harbour the rays of the sun and is a perfect ending for everyday dinners or for crowning a grand banquet.

*Shortcrust pastry should always be homemade. It is relatively easy to succeed: here's how.*

In May, it may be enjoyed topped with strawberries, wild strawberries and cherries. Later in the season, it is sublime with raspberries and apricots (one of my favourites) as well as peaches and any member of the plum family. In autumn, the pear tart and apples are triumphant. A fine flaky apple tart is a sheer delight. To make the pastry, there is a wealth of choices: sweet flan pastry, shortcrust, puff pastry, brioche . . .

Homemade pastry dough is not an operation that is easy to master. It must be tried at least once, just for fun. If you fail for lack of time or practice, it is always possible to buy a ready-made pastry, especially puff pastry, which may be bought frozen and produces perfectly acceptable results.

On the other hand, shortcrust pastry should really be homemade. The recipe is relatively easy – the secret lies in the wrist. To begin, make sure all the ingredients are the same temperature. Do not mix egg yolks straight out of the refrigerator together with softened butter. Most important, do not labour over the dough too much, otherwise the butter will melt.

In a large bowl, mix 7 oz (200g) of flour and 1 1/2 oz (40g) of sifted icing sugar with 1 1/2 oz (40g) of ground almonds. Crush any lumps. Make a well in the middle and pour in 5 1/4 oz (160g) of softened butter, a pinch of salt, 3 1/4 oz (80g) of icing sugar and the seeds from a vanilla pod. To remove them, you must flatten the pod, cutting it lengthwise down the middle and pulling out the seeds with the point of a knife. Mix the ingredients thoroughly together in the well, without incorporating the flour from the sides. Beat 2 egg yolks rapidly into the mixture, but without working the dough too hard. Then cover the mixture with the flour remaining around the sides and mix roughly together. To form a dough, pat the mixture lightly and quickly between your palms, dropping it onto a clean work surface. Repeat this no more than two or three times so that the butter will not melt. Mould the dough into a ball, and set it in a cool place to stiffen for 30 minutes. It may be stored in the refrigerator for one or two days, and for much longer in the freezer. I recommend using icing sugar, as although caster sugar also stores well, it never makes the dough as fine. Also, with icing sugar, the shape of the dough changes less in the course of cooking. The ingredients called for in this recipe are enough to make two tarts for six to eight people; the results are not as good if the recipe is altered for smaller quantities. Since dough keeps so well, it is sensible to make twice as much as necessary. Shortcrust pastry is often cooked before the tart is given its filling.

When the dough has stiffened, spread it out by kneading it with your hand. Once flattened, cut it in two down the middle, keeping one half and saving the other for a subsequent use. Lightly flour the work surface and roll out the dough in as round a shape as you can manage. Using a large plate or, better yet, a pie cutter, cut out a circle and save the trimmings. Pierce the dough with a fork, and put it in the pie tin so that the holes are on the bottom.

Knead the remaining trimmings of dough into a small ball, then roll it little by little into a thin cord of less than 1/4 inch (6 mm) thick until it is long enough to edge the tart. With a brush dipped in water, moisten the edge of the pastry and attach the cord to make a border: with the fingers of your left hand, hold down the interior of the cord while pinching all along the rim with the right thumb and index finger to make a pretty pattern.

Next, leave the tart in the refrigerator for at least 30 minutes. Then bake it for about 20 minutes in an oven that has been preheated to 350°F/180°C/Gas Mark 4. Once cooked, allow the pastry to cool on a wire rack. Then, the only thing left to do is to decorate it with your favourite fruit.

With the remaining dough, you can make little biscuits. Roll the pastry until it is about 1 1/2 inches (4 cm) in diameter. Cut them into slices about 1/2 inch (1 cm) thick, then roll them in granulated sugar. Put them on a buttered baking sheet and bake them in the oven at 350°F/180°C/Gas Mark 4). If you prefer little spiralled biscuits, you can make them with a fluted pastry bag. Make a 1 1/4 inch (3 cm) circle and decorate the top with a glacé cherry. Bake them in the same way. Often, shortcrust pastry is served with red fruit and *crème patissière*, whipped cream, etc. For my part, I prefer to leave tarts made from red fruit unadorned. Their natural flavours are best enhanced by adding just a small spoonful of jam made from the same fruit as the tart.

# Wild Strawberry Shortcrust Tart

**Serves 4**

shortcrust pastry

2 oz (50g) strawberry jam

1 1/4 lb (500g) wild
strawberries

icing sugar

1. Preheat the oven and cook the pastry shell for 20 minutes at 350°F/180°C/Gas Mark 4. Once done, allow it to cool on a wire rack.

2. Heat the jam and sieve it. With a brush, baste the inside of the pie shell with jam. Reserve the rest for glazing the strawberries.

3. Arrange strawberries one by one, point up, along the border of the tart. Then put in the rest of the strawberries, nicely spacing the ones on the surface.

4. With a brush, coat the top of the tart with the remaining jam.

5. Powder the border of the tart with icing sugar, protecting the strawberries with a paper cut-out held in your other hand.

*Enjoy this tart with
a fruity and aromatic wine,
such as a light and rosy
Muscat de Beaumes-de-Venise
(Bernardins domain).*

AUTUMN

# .TRUFFLES.

Since the earliest days of civilization, truffles have been the black diamonds of French cuisine. Inscriptions referring to them have even been found on earthenware tablets. Every imaginable superlative has been bestowed on them: 'Black queen', 'magic potato', 'fragrant nugget', 'black pearl', and so on.

The truffle, whose enchanting perfume is said to have aphrodisiacal powers, has the added allure of mystery. It must be sought out as one of nature's treasures, since it is a plant that cannot be cultivated. A truffle appears at will, near host plants like hazel trees and certain pines, but it is most often found near the truffle-friendly oak. The truffle is partial to particular soil conditions that recall the Tertiary era: a warm, Mediterranean-like climate, free of winter frost, and well sheltered from summer storms. Among the numerous types of truffles, the best and most fragrant is the Tuber melanosporum.

The truffle harvest stretches from the end of November to March. However, they are not so much harvested as hunted, or tracked down. It is an ancestral trade, practised by a *gaveur* or *rabassier,* who should possess a solid knowledge of nature and an inspired flair for truffle hunting. Digging haphazardly in truffle territory is the surest way to destroy everything, since these mushrooms are not hardy like potatoes. One must resort to allies such as pigs, who are blessed with snouts that are sensitive to the black mushroom, a trained dog (often a mongrel) who, unlike the sow, does not devour the truffle, or flies, who attracted by the fragrance, come to lay their eggs there.

You may have strolled through a truffle market, such as the one in Richerenches, in the Vaucluse. There you will find yourself amidst a council of conspirators: the truffles are invisible, but you can smell them, sense them all around, because the whole village is embalmed in their scent. Prices are exchanged like passwords – you either take it or leave it. By noontime, everything is sold, and the truffles have disappeared. Only their perfume persists. Then set off down the road for Mondragon, where in his restaurant Le Beaugravière Guy Julien will initiate you into the subtle marriages of the wines of the

*The writer Colette, a truffle hunter, didn't trust anyone to wash her prized truffles for her.*

Rhône and the truffle, which he uses in scrambled eggs and omelettes. And don't forget to visit Vaison-la-Romaine! These days, the suspect qualities of certain truffles has been the subject of much talk. Trust only reputed merchants, such as the house of Pebeyre in Cahors.

A fresh truffle is firm to the touch, black in colour and veined with white on the interior. If you see a light groove in the mushroom's side, it is a guarantee of quality: it means that the mushroom's texture has been checked and verified. The truffle is a reservoir of fragrance, which escapes in the blink of an eye. You must therefore take precautions and, most importantly, do not expose truffles to open air. They will keep very well in the refrigerator for about 10 days. Before cooking, your first operation is to brush them. The writer Colette, who hunted truffles in Lot, did not entrust this task to anyone else. With the point of a small knife, extract the earth and gravel lodged in the mushroom's cavities. Brush it with a small, moistened brush many times to obtain a perfect cleanliness. Do not let truffles soak, since they hate dampness. You will find it necessary to peel them, as the truffle's interior is superior to its rind. Peel a truffle as you would a potato, peeling as thinly as possible, and reserve the rinds in a bowl, covered with corn oil or grapeseed oil – unflavoured – which you will use later to make an exquisite vinaigrette.

Truffles may be eaten raw or cooked. For salads, slice them into wafer-thin slivers, season them with a little oil and a squeeze of lemon, which is preferable to vinegar, a pinch of Guérande salt and pepper. Mix them either with salad or sliced warm potatoes. When cooked, truffles enrich all manner of sauces.

The purists like truffles by themselves. The most famous recipe remains the truffle *en papillote* cooked in ashes. To do this, envelop each truffle in a thin slice of fat, wrap them in a square of aluminium foil, put it in the centre of the hot cinders of a fire and let them cook for 20 to 25 minutes. Serve them with toasted wholegrain bread, salted butter and a pinch of Guérande salt. The ideal accompaniments to truffles are eggs, pasta,

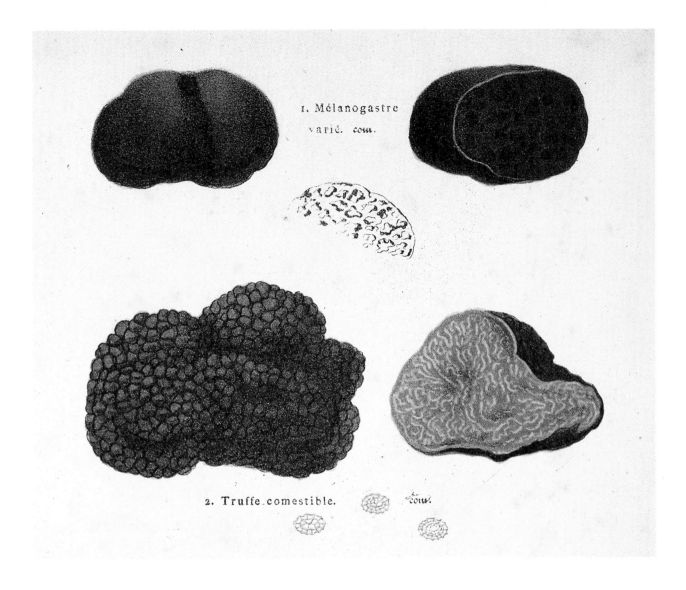

1. Mélanogastre
varié. com.

2. Truffe comestible.

potatoes, meats, and most particularly ham, which perfectly captures and restores the powerful fragrance of this edible jewel. The smoked belly of pork with truffles made by my friend Charles Barrier in Tours is a delight! The fat of a goose or duck, spring onions, onions, leeks and parmesan also bring out the flavour of truffles. As does, most of all, garlic – in small quantities. For an omelette with truffles, begin by rubbing the frying pan with a clove of garlic. Avoid cutting truffles with a knife; crush them with a fork in order to bring the fragrance out of their spores. I find that, when truffles are left in various sizes, they awaken the sensitivity of the palate.

In my restaurant, I like to serve this original recipe of truffles in a galette, or thin pancake, of onions and smoked bacon.

# TRUFFLE AND SMOKED BACON PANCAKES

SERVES 4

**4 large truffles**

**2 cloves garlic**

**4 oz (100g) softened butter**

**11 oz (300g) peeled onions**

**4 oz (100g) goose fat**

**1 1/2 oz (40g) smoked bacon, diced**

**salt and ground pepper**

**4 oz (100g) cream**

**3 leaves of filo pastry**

**Guérande salt**

1. Peel the truffles and slice them wafer-thin.

2. Cut four rounds of greaseproof paper, about 5 inches (13cm) in diameter, and rub them with a clove of garlic. Using a brush, butter them generously. Cover each round with slices of truffles, overlapping them slightly. Butter the surface again. Place the rounds in the refrigerator for at least 1 hour. This step may also be done the night before.

3. Finely slice the onions. Place the goose fat and the diced smoked bacon in a saucepan. Season with salt and pepper. Cook the ingredients for about 10 minutes without allowing them to brown.

4. Add the sliced truffle peelings and let them heat just barely. Add cream and heat for 2 minutes. Season, cover, and set the pan aside, keeping it warm.

5. Cut 12 rounds of filo pastry, each about 5 inches (13cm) in diameter. Place a round of pastry on a baking sheet and brush it with a fine film of butter. Place another round on top of it and repeat, topping it with a third round. Do not butter the surface. Prepare a total of four in this way. Slide the baking sheet into the oven which has been preheated to 400-425°F/200-220°C/(Gas Mark 6-7) and bake them for 8 to 10 minutes until they are lightly golden.

6. Take the rounds out of the oven, spreading the onions, smoked bacon and sliced truffle peelings on top while the pastry is still hot.

7. Take the rounds of sliced truffles out of the refrigerator and arrange them on top of the galette. Leave the paper on top.

8. Slide the rounds back into the warm oven, just long enough to melt the butter that seals the truffles together. The truffles should be warm.

9. Take the sheet out of the oven, and remove the papers.

10. Season the tops with Guérande salt and a turn of the pepper mill. Serve with toasted wholegrain bread that has been rubbed with garlic.

*Serve with*
*a Corton-Charlemagne*
*for real fireworks!*

# .OYSTERS.

The oyster is the pearl of the seas. Adored by the Chinese and Romans, exalted by the Greeks, it is an ancestral treat. This hermaphroditic bivalve mollusc is high in nutritive value, and its dietetic qualities make it a precious component of alimentary equilibrium. It has few calories, and so is not fattening. Apart from that, oysters whet the appetite, encourage sleep and are even said to provoke the ardours of Venus.

There are two kinds of oysters: the French oyster, which is flat and rounded, and the oyster that comes from the Pacific, which is cupped and almost rectangular. The latter has replaced Portugese oysters, which were decimated by an epidemic. Among flat oysters is the famous Belon, which is raised in the deep pure water of the Belon river, the Bouziges of the ponds of Thau, the Gravette from Arcachon and, rarest of all, the Marennes that come from Brittany or Arachon. The incomparable flavour of oysters, large or small, may be enjoyed raw or cooked.

You should buy live oysters with tightly shut shells. If you buy them in a hamper, check the expiry date on the label. Be cautious about those labels which only state the date of packaging. Make sure the oysters are tightly shut, or at least that they close immediately if you touch them. Their shells should be moist and the oysters should feel heavy in your hand, weighed down with all their rich sea water.

Oysters should be prepared immediately. If you must keep them, stack them flat side down. Wrap them in a wet cloth, put them in the bottom of the refrigerator, and put a weight on top of them to prevent them from opening. The best temperature is 46°F (8°C). Oysters do not like very cold temperatures and a frozen oyster is a lost oyster. They should be opened at the last minute, an operation which requires a certain technique. In particular, you must avoid breaking their lobes and must detach the thin muscle which may remain stuck to the larger shell. Once they are open, check the quality of the oysters by poking the beard or the cilia, which should retract immediately. If you find that you

*Purists like oysters raw, seasoned with ground pepper. But oysters may also be cooked. Jump right in!*

must wait before serving oysters, which often happens at a party, replace the top shell on each oyster and pile them on top of one another. Cover them with a damp towel and put them in the refrigerator or outside, as long as they won't freeze.

There are many ways to enjoy raw oysters. Purists like them plain, with a sprinkling of ground pepper, and reject both lemons and the famous shallot vinaigrette. Personally, I prefer them with a squeeze of lemon, which makes them more digestible. You may also serve them as they are done in southwestern France, accompanied by foie gras on toast, or *crépinettes* (small flat sausages), as Robert Courtine suggests. And, of course, oysters are wonderful served with finely sliced rye bread spread with salted butter.

Oysters may also be cooked. This is not, as many believe, an invention of the so-called nouvelle cuisine. To the contrary, in the past, they were more often served cooked and still warm. Jump right in, but whatever the recipe, choose fleshy and milky flat or cupped oysters.

Open the oysters carefully and strain the juice into a saucepan. Add white wine or champagne (one third of the volume of the oysters' water) and a little finely chopped shallot. Add pepper, but not salt. Bring to the boil, let it simmer for 2 or 3 minutes, and strain the juice. Place the shelled oysters side by side in a generously buttered plate and pour the juice mixed with wine on top. Allow the dish to simmer and turn the oysters one by one, removing them 30 seconds later. Make sure they do not boil, or else they will overcook. Once they have been poached it is best to trim them since, in the course of cooking, the beards become hard and disagreeable to eat. To the cooking juices, add another third of the total volume of white wine or champagne along with an equal amount of *crème fraîche*. Reduce it until you have a velvety sauce. Finish by whisking in small pieces of chilled butter. Place the oysters back in the shells, which have been washed and dried. Let them warm for a few moments in the oven, then take them out and cover them with the sauce. If you would like to cook them *au*

gratin, add a large spoonful of whisked *crème fraîche* to the sauce at the last minute, pour the sauce over the oysters and let them glaze just for a moment under the grill. It is a very rapid process, and the sauce should be lightly golden. You may add garnishings of cooked vegetables, fennel, spinach, courgettes, mushrooms, asparagus, leeks, endives, etc, as well as adding a hint of curry powder or saffron to the sauce.

Another simpler preparation that is just as delicious is to simply poach the oysters in their filtered juices with a little butter and then season them with a little melted butter with lemon juice and chives. Poached in this way, oysters may also be breaded and fried or served with pasta, fish or meats such as duck, as the famed Claude Terrail serves them at the Tour d'Argent. They may also be served shelled, in bowls or in shallow porcelain plates, as in the following recipe. This is a far cry from a simple platter of shellfish!

# WARM OYSTERS
# WITH FENNEL AND CURRY

SERVES 1

**6 cupped oysters**

**1 small shallot, finely chopped**

**3 1/2 fl oz (100 ml) white**

**wine**

**1 1/4 oz (30g) butter**

**1/3 medium-sized onion**

**1/4 small bulb of fennel,**

**chopped**

**2 tablespoons crème fraîche**

**pinch of curry powder**

**salt and pepper**

**1 small spoonful salmon roe**

**chopped chives**

1. Open the oysters on the muscle side.

2. Strain their liquid through a sieve lined with a fine cloth that has been soaked in cold water.

3. In a casserole or saucepan, place the finely chopped shallot, white wine and a knob of butter. Bring to the boil and reduce by half.

4. Generously butter a flameproof dish, then place the shelled oysters in it side by side. Pour the oysters' juice into the wine and shallot sauce. Bring the sauce back to the boil and then pour it through a sieve onto the oysters. Place the dish over medium heat. After 30 seconds, turn the oysters one by one. When they begin to simmer, remove them from the heat immediately.

5. Arrange the oysters in a dish. Let them cool a bit and then trim their beards with small scissors.

6. Allow the chopped onion and fennel to sweat in butter for 3 minutes. Add the oysters' cooking liquid.

7. Pour in 2 generous spoonfuls of *crème fraîche* and a hint of curry powder. Bring to the boil and let it reduce as it continues to boil lightly for 5 or 6 minutes. Season.

8. Strain the sauce, then add the rest of the butter. Whisk, then place the oysters back in the sauce for a few seconds to reheat them.

9. Arrange them in a warmed dish, and add 1 spoonful of salmon roe to the sauce. Stir the sauce and pour it over the oysters. Sprinkle with chopped chives.

*Serve with*
*a balanced and elegant white*
*Châteauneuf-du-Pape.*

# .SCALLOPS.

This noble mollusc, encased in its striated shell, comes from the bottom of the sea and, like the white wine of the monks, it has a religious origin. The scallop was named by religious pilgrims in fustian robes who voyaged on foot to St Jacques-de-Compostella, whose distinctive emblem was a pearly scallop shell which came from the coasts of Galicia.

In France scallop fishing is strictly regulated, because the species is endangered and the demand is enormous. To ensure the survival of this delicate gourmet gem, the office of Maritime Affairs fixes draconian quotas according to the depletion of stock and the size of the shells.

Once out of their shells, scallops are a delight, with an extremely subtle, slightly sugary flavour. Scallops lend themselves to a multitude of preparations which respect their subtle fragrance. Never mask or dominate the scallop's flavour with strong-tasting ingredients – judge proportions carefully. You can recognize a good scallop by its heaviness. It should be shut tightly (an open-shelled scallop will have lost its freshness) and the mollusc inside should be alive; its flesh should be firm and translucent white in colour. The best are those without coral. Even if the coral is beautiful, large and perfectly edible, it will have spoilt the flavour of the scallop.

It is best to entrust the fishmonger with the job of opening the shell; he or she will insert a knife blade between the top and bottom shell, separate the membranes and the beard and remove the scallop's blackish pouch. It is important to wash scallops well and never to let them soak, lest they lose their taste. They may be stored for a short time in a clean cloth. Do not leave them for long, even if they are kept chilled, and avoid buying them already shelled and packaged in plastic.

You can prepare this divine

*How should*

*you prepare the*

*lovely scallop?*

*As naturally*

*as can be.*

mollusc for eating raw or cooked. Cut into two or three thin slices, the raw scallop may be added to salads or an instant marinade composed of a little olive oil flavoured with a touch of saffron and seasoned well with cider vinegar, lemon, Guérande salt and pepper. I serve four scallops per person, cut into rounds if they are large. Scallops may be cooked in almost any way, except, in my opinion, steamed, which makes them shrink. To keep them flavourful, the best way is to cook them at the last possible moment before gathering at table, and as lightly as possible.

A simple and natural way to prepare scallops is to cut the flesh into two or three slivers, butter them well and place them back in their shell seasoned with salt (from Guérande if possible), pepper and a piece of fresh thyme. Place them in the oven for a few minutes. Finish with a light squeeze of lemon. Cooked this way, scallops retain all their flavour without any unnecessary embellishments.

Scallops may also be grilled on the barbecue, basted with olive oil, thyme and a hint of curry powder, and may be accompanied by classic sauces (like *beurre blanc* or hollandaise) or, for a more modern twist, a butter sauce seasoned with soya sauce. Alternatively, you may prefer to prepare them as kebabs with mushrooms and smoked bacon.

In my opinion, coating scallops with flour to fry them is a mistake, because it masks their subtle flavour. I advise simply frying them in butter after seasoning them with salt and pepper. Add chopped shallots and parsley if you like, as is done in Bordeaux, or garlic and parsley in Mediterranean fashion. When I prepare scallops for my family, I prefer to fry them briefly in olive oil, then season them with Guérande salt and ground pepper and serve them with a salad of endives sliced finely lengthwise, the simplest preparation in the world. A few ounces of shellfish for the pleasure of the taste buds…

Scallop kebab with mushrooms and smoked bacon.

# BRAISED SCALLOPS

SERVES 4

**4 oz (100g) butter**

**12–16 large scallops**

**coarse salt and crushed peppercorns**

FOR THE SAUCE

**3 1/2 fl oz (100ml) stock made**
**with the trimmed scallop beards**

**8 fl oz (250ml) crème fleurette**

**2 oz (50g) butter**

**2 fl oz (50ml) lemon juice**

**1 teaspoon (5g) blanched lemon zest**

**1/4 bundle of chives**

1. Butter four dishes. Cut the scallops into rounds. In the bottom of each dish, arrange 12 rounds. Butter them, then place a half-peppercorn and 2 grains of coarse salt on each.

2. Reduce the scallop stock by half. Add the *crème fleurette*. Reduce, then emulsify with the butter and incorporate the lemon juice. Add the lemon zest.

3. Place the dishes in the oven for about 3 minutes, then cover the scallops with the sauce. Add a hint of finely chopped chives on each scallop.

*Serve with*
*a white wine from Burgundy,*
*such as Puligny-Montrachet or*
*Chassagne-Montrachet*

# .HERRING.

The herring, that fish of the cold seas, has over the centuries decided the destinies of empires. This white gold of the sea has provoked wars and rivalries. It has been used as ransoms, as gifts and as currency, just as spices were. It has nourished entire populations, thanks to its celebrated prolificacy.

The English who fished herring commercially dubbed it King Herring. This silver-bellied pelagic fish of the Clupeidae family lives in massed schools which, in passage, destroy everything in their path. Herrings feed on plankton, which make them one of the cod's favourite dishes. Fishing is regulated by quotas laid down by the European Community, and the major French ports for herring are Boulogne, Fécamp and Dieppe. The latter is known as the capital of Clupeidae since, on 11 November each year, the herring is fêted there, as well it should be.

Herring is caught by trawling, but the best fish are captured in a net derived from the seine used on rowing boats for inshore fishing. Curiously, the herring has been neglected in recent times, even though it used to be a much sought-after, princely prize. It is during the autumn months that you must savour this fresh and inexpensive fish, which is as much a gourmet pleasure as bass, turbot or John Dory. All you need to know is how to make the most of it. It is in autumn, in fact, that the fish is heavy with milt or roe, and therefore its gustatory qualities are at their best. From January onwards, after mating, their flesh is drier, and they are described as 'shotten' or 'spent'. In the spawning season, in early winter, the seasides were once white with roe and silvery scales.

You will recognize a good herring by its firmness, shiny scales and bright red eyes and gills. Take care when choosing: the herring does not keep well and the loss of scales is a sign that it has begun to spoil. The full herring may be recog-

*In England, herring is sometimes referred to as King Herring. Discover its soft white milt, meltingly light and subtle to the taste.*

nized by its round, thick flanks, while if it is empty, its belly is compressed. Small, full herring are the best. Herring is sold uncleaned – the fishmonger should gut and clean it without damaging the milt in the males and the roe if the fish is female.

To prepare fresh herring, scale it simply by wiping it once or twice with a cloth. Empty it via its gills without damaging the roe. Wash it rapidly and dry. If it is to be cooked whole, make little incisions along its back every 1/2–3/4 inch (1–2 cm) on both sides to facilitate cooking and to permit the fat to ooze out, since herring is a fatty fish. You may also ask the fishmonger to fillet it. There are many ways to enjoy this fish which is all too often scorned: marinated, fried, poached, grilled, cooked in the oven, in a papillote, braised with a cream sauce or mustard sauce and accompanied by seasonal vegetables, cabbage, leeks, potatoes, and so on.

The most famous recipe for fresh herring is marinated *à la dieppoise*. Prepare a court-bouillon with vinegar, white wine, aromatic vegetables, herbs and seasoning. Boil it for at least 30 minutes. Scale, trim and clean the herrings, without touching the milt or roe. Poach them for about 10 minutes in the court-bouillon without allowing them to boil. Let them cool in their marinade, then place them in the refrigerator until you are ready to serve them. My preferences lean to two simple preparations: grilled or simply cooked in the oven. Scale and clean them, always leaving the milt or roe intact, make the small incisions described above and roll the herrings in oil and grill them. Coat them with mustard and finish cooking them in a low oven. Alternatively, after you make the incisions, place them on a bed of coarse sea salt on a dish and cook them in a hot oven. Serve with unpeeled potatoes, salted butter, melted butter or a mustard sauce. As for variations on the mustard sauce, try a mustard hollandaise or, more economical, a reduction of shallots and white wine mixed with a light *béchamel* and mustard. All of them are good!

Every year, my friend Jean Delaveyne and I attend the herring festival at Dieppe. We return with bags brimming with plump herrings, which was one of the first specialities that contributed to the reputation of my restaurant in its early days. Many people do not recall the taste of herrings cooked with their milt and roe. I love herrings – particularly the milt. The following recipe is the ideal preparation for savouring the herring's white, subtle, tasty milt.

Fresh herring marinated *à la dieppoise*, recipe p.102.

# HERRING MILT WITH VERJUICE

SERVES 4

1 1/4 lb (500g) fresh herring milt

3 1/2 fl oz (100ml) spirit vinegar

4 oz (100g) butter

oil, flour, sprigs of parsley, salt
and freshly ground pepper

3 1/4 oz (80g) button mushrooms, diced

3 1/4 oz (80g) tart apples, diced

3/4 oz (20g) top-quality capers

3 1/4 oz (80g) tomato,
skinned, seeded and diced

2 fl oz (50ml) verjuice

2 fl oz (50ml) cider vinegar

1. Put the sacs of milt to soak for an hour in cold water with the spirit vinegar. Then remove the blood-tinged filament with the point of a small knife.

2. Drain the milt and dry carefully with a piece of kitchen towel.

3. Put a handful of flour on a plate and sprinkle it lightly on the milt.

4. With a fine needle, pierce the sacs of milt lightly in five or six places so they will not burst while cooking.

5. In a frying pan, heat slightly less than half the butter with a drop of olive oil. Carefully place the milt in the pan, season it and fry it lightly. Remove from the heat, place on a warm dish, and put in a warm oven.

6. Add the rest of the butter to the saucepan, along with the mushrooms. Sauté them briskly, then add the apples. Season them and finish browning them. Add the capers and the diced tomatoes and stir just until they are heated.

7. Pour the above garnish and the cooking butter on the milt. Sprinkle with sprigs of parsley. Deglaze the frying pan with the verjuice and cider vinegar and pour them over the milt and the garnish.

*Serve with a white Sancerre
like Lucien Crochet's Clos du Chêne Marchand,
a wine that is fresh, vivacious,
and full of subtlety.*

# .CEPS.

Autumn is mushroom season. They enchant the uninitiated, arouse the interest of scientists, cheer nature-lovers and delight the palates of gastronomes. You will find the cep nestled among moss, ferns and the undergrowth. Dubbed the king of mushrooms, proclaimed by Nero to be 'the flesh of Gods', the cep is venerated by gourmets for the delicacy of its white flesh and its woody, lightly nutty flavour.

Four species make up the Boletus family. They are, in order of importance and demand: the Bordeaux cep, with its brownish-ochre top, the musk-scented bronze cep, the pine cep, recognizable by its mahogany colour, and finally the seasonal cep, a summer mushroom, which is pale at the base and bordered by a white rim. Ceps come mainly from the Southwest, Auvergne, Sologne and Alsace. Though they are relatively expensive in Paris, they are more reasonably priced in the provinces due to the large number of vendors.

These de luxe mushrooms should be handled delicately. First, as with all mushrooms, they must be fresh. They are always better when young (the littlest ones are called champagne corks) and must be eaten without delay. Waiting will kill their flavour. If they cannot be eaten immediately, put them in the refrigerator; avoid piling them cap down, because any maggots they carry will be tempted to nestle there. Be careful: if ceps are stored too long, they can become toxic. Check them carefully and throw away any that are less than fresh. When preparing ceps, cut off any blemishes and traces of dirt on the base. Cut off the stalk just under the cap of the mushroom and peel the caps. If they are too soft or in dubious shape, do not keep them. Likewise, if the stalks are spongy, viscous or of a deep green colour, discard them. They will ruin

*Ceps are also known as the 'flesh of the Gods'. When prepared with warm foie gras, eating them is, as Alain Chapel said, 'to taste the truth'.*

the dish. Naturally rich in water, these mushrooms should not be washed, since they will lose their aroma. It will suffice to wipe them gently with a damp cloth or paper towel. Using a little brush with semi-stiff bristles, remove any debris. If they are very soiled rinse them briskly under running water, then dry them with a cloth.

One source of never-ending controversy is over the question of whether ceps should be blanched in boiling water before they are cooked or not. In my opinion, doing so makes them lose their fine nutty taste. You will discover that ceps possess different nuances of flavour according to the way you choose to cut them, whether escaloped, sliced or diced. It is the same phenomenon you will find with potatoes, whether they are fried, cut into matchsticks or cooked *Pont-Neuf.* If the ceps are the small 'champagne cork' type, I prefer to cook them whole or in 1/4 inch (6 mm) slices. When cooking, ceps may be sautéed in the frying pan to make a fricassée, prepared in cream sauce or grilled in groundnut oil, as is done in my native region of Poitou. They are wonderful in an omelette, or with fresh pasta. Otherwise, you can use them to reinforce a sauce with a red wine base, in a stew or as a garnish for braised meat or poultry, calves' kidneys, pork or freshwater fish.

Here is one rustic way to prepare ceps: choose medium-sized ones and cut the stalk just under their caps. In a frying pan, heat a little olive oil and gently brown the caps. Season them. Dice the stalks and a little raw ham, and finely chop some shallots. Then melt a knob of butter in a frying pan and add the ceps, the ham and shallots. Season with pepper (the ham is already salty enough). Cook the mixture gently and add chopped parsley. Garnish the mushrooms caps with this mixture and put them in a gratin dish. Sprinkle each cap with breadcrumbs (the best are crumbled brioche fried in butter). Place the mushrooms in the oven for a few minutes to brown.

The aromatic ingredients that go best with ceps are shallot, flat parsley, fresh walnuts, olive oil, goose or duck fat, and a dash of saffron and vermouth. Use garlic only with extreme moderation, because it smothers the delicate flavour of the ceps. Jean Delaveyne, whom many of us consider to be the Van Gogh of cuisine, is a great mushroom specialist, and he prepares a wonderful recipe for ceps, in his *mille-choux*, a happy mingling of ceps enhanced in flavour by a little kirsch. If the ceps are very fresh, you may also slice them finely into an autumnal salad, enriched with a lemon and olive oil vinaigrette and sprinkled with walnuts or fresh slivered almonds. I do not care for tinned ceps, because they often lose their firmness and become slimy. The season is short, ending in mid November, so you must make the most of it. One of the best combinations remains warm *foie gras* and ceps – delicious! Renowned chef Alain Chapel used to refer to this preparation as '*Manger la verité*': to eat truth itself.

# CEPS SAUTÉED
# IN FOIE GRAS OF DUCK

SERVES 4

**4 medium-sized firm ceps**

**2 tablespoons goose**
**or duck fat**

**salt, pepper, coarse salt and**
**crushed peppercorns**

**4 slices of raw foie gras of**
**duck, about 4 oz (100g) each**

**2 fl oz (50ml) wine vinegar**

**7 fl oz (200ml) chicken stock**

**1 sprig of parsley, finely**
**chopped**

1. Carefully clean the ceps without getting them wet, cut them into slices about 1/4 inch (6 mm) thick and then season with salt and pepper.

2. In a large frying pan, melt 1 tablespoon of duck or goose fat and sauté the ceps until they are lightly browned.

3. Drain the ceps and arrange them on a warm plate kept in the oven.

4. Season the foie gras with coarse salt and crushed peppercorns. Add a little more fat to the frying pan and brown the slices of foie gras for about 2 minutes on each side. Take them off the heat and place them on a paper towel.

5. Discard the fat and deglaze the frying pan with the wine vinegar.

6. Pour the warm chicken stock on the ceps, arrange them on top of the foie gras and sprinkle them with the warm vinegar sauce. Finally, sprinkle the platter with the chopped parsley.

*Serve with a solid,*
*full Pomerol, such as*
*Château-Trotanoy.*

# .FOIE GRAS.

Foie gras is the star product of French cuisine, as indispensable for a party as champagne. For the Route du Rhum 1990 race, Philippe Poupon, the skipper of Fleury-Michon IX, asked me to prepare his meals, imposing on me only one condition: foie gras on board!

An obligatory presence at holidays and parties, foie gras becomes more expensive each year. Why not try to prepare it yourself? If you follow my instructions, it is not a very complicated exercise. Should it be goose or duck? These are two products with very different tastes: everyone has his or her preference.

For cold liver terrine, I favour goose liver, on account of its greater subtlety of flavour. Duck liver, which is more bitter and has a coarser fragrance, is more difficult to work with but is superior to goose liver should you decide to serve it warm.

The first imperative is to choose an impeccable piece of liver. A good raw liver is identified by separating the two lobes. If they break apart the liver is too fat, and it will melt while cooking. If, on the other hand, they appear elastic, they will be dry and have little aroma after cooking. The ideal liver will be supple, stretchy and taut until it breaks cleanly. The colour is also important. Do not buy livers that are a dull grey, or those that have green traces of bile or red marbling from blood. Choose instead livers that are an off-white colour, bordering on yellow. If you need a number of them to fill your terrine, choose livers of an identical colour. Check the freshness of the livers, which should be smooth, with an agreeable, unpronounced odour. Foie gras of duck should weigh about 14 oz–1 1/2 lb (400–600g) and goose liver should weigh about 1 1/4–1 3/4 lb (500–800g). They may be found year round, but November is the best season. As the holidays approach, the best livers are snapped up quickly, and their prices are sky-high.

The most classic preparation of foie gras is in a terrine. Your first operation should be to remove the blood that remains in the veins. With a knife, cut a band of 1/2–3/4 inch (1–2 cm) around the perimeter of the larger lobe. Then leave it to soak in the refrigerator for a

*November is the time to buy fresh liver. Here is how to choose and prepare it.*

half-day in salted iced water: with the salt's help, the water will penetrate the liver and remove the blood. When you are ready to make the terrine, separate the two lobes, removing the green traces of bile and the fine film of skin which covers the liver. With a small knife, cut out the main vein that runs through the liver. Should the vein break, leave the liver as it is. You must undertake this operation at room temperature and not cool the liver too much, or else it will break apart.

Season the liver the night before you cook it. Foie gras is never better than just plain with a little bit of salt, pepper and spices. It is thus that it displays such a delicate taste. In my opinion, truffles, port, madeira and cognac denature and smother the liver's own taste. The liver should be well-salted, about 1/4 oz per lb (15g per kilo), and seasoned with a pinch of pepper, a hint of mace, *quatre épices* (a traditional French spice which contains equal parts of ground ginger, nutmeg, white pepper and cloves) and a teaspoon of sugar, which will prevent the liver from blackening and preserve its pretty rosy colour. In order to make sure the seasoning is even, place the spices in a dish, mix them well, then dip in the liver, adding, if you absolutely must, 2 teaspoons of wine or *eau-de-vie*. Place the liver in the refrigerator for 8 to 12 hours, covered with a sheet of clingfilm, taking care to turn it two or three times. The seasoning, with the sugar, will preserve the liver's colour (this is a process well known to butchers).

Next, put the liver in a terrine. Place the big lobe in the bottom of the terrine, with the smooth part facing down – by virtue of its volume, it will resist the rising heat better. Cover with the smaller lobe, which should also be placed smooth-side down. Fill in any holes with the little pieces you trimmed off at the beginning in order to remove the blood. Cover with greaseproof paper, not aluminium foil, which will blacken the top of the terrine. Preheat the oven to 250°F/120°C/Gas Mark 1/2 and prepare a bain-marie at 176°F (80°C). The temperature should be exact – do not rely on guesswork. Use a cooking thermometer, since liver hates excessive heat – this will be the secret of your success. Put the terrine in the bain-marie; the water should rise to about 3/4 inch (2 cm) from the edge of the larger container to obtain a good distribution of heat. Allow 60 minutes' cooking time for goose liver and 50 minutes for duck liver. If you prolong the cooking time, the liver may melt. On the other hand, if it is not cooked enough, it will not cut well and the liver will be disgusting. Personally, I prefer liver well-cooked rather than raw, contrary to the winds of fashion.

Once it is done, take the liver out of the oven and let it cool for 2 or 3 hours at room temperature. Before the fat hardens, clarify it to remove the blood which might have spread. Whisk it in order to blanch it, then replace it on the terrine. Then place on the terrine a small board of the same size and add weights. Place all of it in the refrigerator. The terrine may be enjoyed 3 or 4 days later, a delay which will improve its taste and texture. It may also be stored chilled for about 10 days. But serve the terrine at room temperature, accompanied by toasted wholemeal bread (it may even be slightly burnt) or with a good baguette. I'm not a fan of brioche and sliced bread. Do not forget to put coarse ground pepper on the side of the plate, as it enhances the rich flavours: liver is a concentrate of perfumes.

LES FOIES GRAS

Extraction de Foies

HISTOIRE ANECDOTIQUE DE L'ALIMENTATION

Éditée spécialement pour la maison Louit Frères & C.º

# WARM FOIE GRAS
# WITH LENTIL CREAM SAUCE

SERVES 4

**4 slices of raw foie gras,
about 4 oz (100g) each**

**7 oz (200g) green lentils**

**4 oz (100g) smoked belly
of pork**

**18 fl oz (500 ml) chicken
stock**

**1/2 pint (300ml) cream**

**1 1/4 oz (30g) small onions**

**1 tablespoon goose fat**

FOR THE AROMATIC GARNISH

**2 cloves of garlic**

**1/2 onion**

**1 small carrot**

**1 clove**

**1 bouquet garni**

**salt and pepper**

**sprigs of chervil**

1. Envelop each slice of foie gras with clingfilm and keep it in the refrigerator.

2. Blanch the lentils, then refresh them. Cook them in water with the aromatic garnish and smoked belly of pork. Season.

3. When the lentils are done, remove the garnish and smoked belly of pork and reserve about 1 oz (25g). Pass the rest of the lentils through the food processor, along with the cooking juices.

4. Heat the resulting purée over a low heat and thin it with the chicken stock. Add the cream and mix well. Pass through a sieve.

5. Mince the small onions and cook them in the goose fat without allowing them to brown.

6. Cut the smoked belly of pork into little pieces and add them to the onions. Put them in the warm sauce, along with the lentils you have reserved.

7. Steam the livers for 8 minutes. Unwrap and drain them. Place each liver in a dish and cover it with the lentil cream sauce and garnish. Sprinkle with sprigs of chervil.

*Serve with a Gewurztraminer Vendanges Tardives
for its power and its mellow harmony.*

# .YOUNG PARTRIDGE.

Appreciated by gourmets, yearling partridge is flavourful and much sought-after game. A very young, un-speckled partridge is known as a *pouillard* in France. For a number of reasons, the partridge is becoming rare.

There are several types of partridge, two of which are found widely through-out France: the red and the grey par-tridge. There is also the rock partridge, which is plumper than the red one, but the two are often confused. It is very rare, and may be found in the Alps and southern regions. Similar in many ways to the *chukar*, it was introduced to restock the supply of game birds. Monogamous and sedentary, partridge pairs often stay together outside the mating season. Some prefer places that are exposed (such as stubble fields, ploughed fields and hedges) while others prefer the edge of the woods and sometimes even perch on low branches. All par-tridges have in common a low, straight, hurried flight and noiseless ground movement when nothing is present to worry them. When being chased, the partridge flees with surprising speed. It is also an indefatigable walker.

From afar, it is very difficult to distinguish a red par-tridge from a grey one; side by side, they have the same silhouette. However, the adult red partridge is a little plumper than the grey. Apart from their difference in size, the general coloration of their plumage is not the same. The red partridge (Alectoris rufa), which is more common in the south and southwest of France, has a red back and stomach; its beak and feet are also red. Its white throat is encircled by a large black band.  The grey partridge (Perdix perdix), which is more abundant to the north of the Loire, has a red-grey tone on its back and is cinder-grey on its stomach, with dark markings in the shape of a horseshoe on the chest. Its beak and feet are grey-blue. The young partridge may be distinguished from an adult by inspecting the tips of its first two wing quills. These primary feathers are pointed and do not moult before the age of approximately 15 months. The feathers that grow back are rounded. This provides a convenient means of judging their age: if the feathers are pointed, dark brown and intact, you have a young par-tridge. If the feathers are still pointed, clear brown and

*To conserve its flavour, young partridge must be cooked with a drop of its blood.*

V-shaped and are obviously not newly grown, the partridge is a yearling. Rounded feathers indicate an adult of two years or more. Another distinctive sign: the young grey partridge possesses a dark beak, which becomes lighter and lighter as the bird ages. To me, the par-tridge is, along with the woodcock, the best feathered game. Or at least it was – since it has been farm-raised it has lost its flavour.

Young partridge should be savoured simply roasted. I find this is the best method, since the flesh is so ten-der. Once it has developed muscles, partridge should be prepared in other ways. The best will be *en chartreuse*, with cabbage. This excellent recipe can be found in any cookbook.

The spit is the ideal way to roast young partridge, as it is for all feathered game. But whatever method you use, partridge should be cooked with a drop of its blood to preserve its flavour. As with all simple culinary proce-dures, roasting a partridge takes careful attention. Once the bird is plucked, flambéed and cleaned, remove the nerves from the thighs. Then truss it and cover its breast with a light coating of fat, without any vine leaves, even those culled from the vines of *grands crus*. Season with salt and pepper, inside and out. Put it in a little roasting dish with a knob of butter and a sprig of fresh thyme.

Cook the partridge for 12 minutes in a warm oven, turning it from time to time. Untruss it, take the fat off the breast, and place it on its back to finish roasting for 6 to 8 minutes. The flesh should be rosy. When you take it out of the oven, season it again and, with the point of a knife, make a small incision between the thigh and the body of the bird so as to allow for a small drop of lemon, and a little salt and pepper. With a little Cognac and a spoonful of water, deglaze the roasting pan. Savour the partridge ador-ned with its bard, in its own juice, with a slice of toast and fried muscat grapes (see page 80). It is a delight, filled with all the fla-vours of autumn.

# SUPREME OF YOUNG PARTRIDGE WITH CABBAGE AND FOIE GRAS

SERVES 4

**4 young partridges, plucked,
flambéed and cleaned**

**8 cabbage leaves**

**8 escalopes of raw foie gras of duck,
about 3/4 oz (20g) each**

**8 thin slices of smoked bacon**

**Guérande salt**

**crushed white peppercorns**

**chopped chives**

1. Remove the sinews and cut off the thighs of the birds. Set aside the suprêmes.

2. Blanch the cabbage leaves in boiling salted water for 1 minute. Cool them and drain them on a cloth. Cut off the end of the large central rib.

3. To make a papillote, lightly flatten a leaf of cabbage. Salt and pepper both sides of a suprême and place it on the leaf. Place a slice of foie gras on top of it. Fold the meats into the leaf, closing it firmly and being careful to keep the foie gras on top. Wrap the papillote with a piece of smoked bacon and enclose the bundle in cling-film, again making sure the foie gras remains on top.

4. Cook the papillotes in a steamer for 15 minutes.

5. Unwrap the papillotes. Place the stuffed cabbage leaves on plates, sprinkling some salt, pepper and chives on top. If you wish, you may fry the thighs and serve them on a little salad as a second dish.

*Serve with
a full-bodied Pomerol.*

# .PHEASANT.

The majestic pheasant is one of the most fascinating birds of the forest, and is a game very much appreciated by gourmets for the flavour of its flesh. Its name comes from the Latin *phasianus*, which was derived from the Greek *Phasianos*, which means 'originating in Phasis', a town in Colchis.

The pheasant probably originated in China and neighbouring regions. It is thought that the Argonauts, who were engaged in the quest for the Golden Fleece under the leadership of Jason, were the means of its introduction to Europe. Pheasants are said to have been captured on the banks of the river Phasis, which ran through ancient Colchis, situated to the south of the Caucasus. According to myth, the Argonauts took the birds home with them to Greece. Then the Romans, after the fall of Greece, distributed pheasants throughout the empire, where they were very highly valued. Emperor Heliogabalus, famed for his follies, fed pheasants to his lions. Vitellus forced an entire province to contribute to one sole course of his dinner: the brains of 500 pheasants.

The male is called a cock, the female is a hen. Up to the age of one or two months, the bird is known as a

*There is nothing better than pheasant roasted on the spit.*

*faisandeau.* Then it is called a young pheasant until it acquires the plumage of an adult. It would be impossible to describe here all the varieties and different plumages of the pheasant.

The impassive, noble cock is remarkable for his striking colouring. His plump tapered body, prolonged by long, impressive tail feathers, is supported by feet adorned with spurs. His relatively long neck stretches to a short, round head, with distinct colours and upright ears, colourful cheeks and, most of all, a beak shaped like that of an eagle. He is a beautiful beast! The hen, on the other hand, is less richly adorned. Her silhouette is finer, her tail is shorter, her fine feet are barren of spurs, with some exceptions. While she has less radiant plumage, the hen has more tender and flavourful flesh. The prettiest feathers don't necessarily make the best game! Determining the age of an adult pheasant is not easy – only very old birds with faded plumage may be easily identified. On the larger parts of the body, the feathers that seem as though they should be those of the cock may appear on the hens, while tufts of rather discoloured beige feathers may turn up on certain males. Generally, the

young pheasant will have grey feet. The infallible sign of youth is ascertained by examining the extremity of the last long tail feather, which will still be pointed rather than the rounded shape you will find on an older bird.

I recommend leaving the bird unplucked for two or three days after you buy it in order to obtain a judicious *faisandage*, or hanging. However, be sure to check the condition of the bird. If it has obvious wounds or if it is wet it must be plucked without delay, especially if the hunter has carried it around in his game pouch for a long time. Don't forget that when you buy the pheasant at market it may have been dead for two days, and sometimes longer. If it is cooked at the correct moment of *faisandage*, pheasant makes a savoury and tender dish, lightly stimulating and easily digested.

Gypsies had a particular way of preparing pheasant. They packed it in clay and cooked it in this hermetically sealed shell. When they broke open the baked shell, the bird's feathers remained stuck to the clay. This preparation

is called *à la gitane*, or in gypsy style, a method which also serves well for cooking hedgehog!

This original recipe aside, the pheasant should be plucked before it is prepared. Put it in the refrigerator for a few hours before plucking to facilitate the procedure. Do not hesitate to flambé it to rid the bird of all traces of down and small feathers, particularly on the wings. Do not forget to remove the tendons from its feet. To do so, make an incision along the length of its foot and, using a trussing needle, take out the tendons that appear. Use pliers, if necessary. Clean the bird carefully and truss it with string.

Methods of cooking pheasant are numerous and often very complicated. I find many recipes to be overcomplicated and somewhat unenticing because they rob the bird of its flavour. I think there is nothing better than a young cock, or hen, roasted in the oven or, even better, on the spit. I like to serve them with boiled endives that are then stewed in the juices of the bird. Meanwhile, if the bird is a little older, it can be served in a ragout, with cabbage, or perhaps in a pie.

# PHEASANT AND FOIE GRAS PIE

1. Slice and set aside 4 oz (100g) of pheasant flesh. Dice the rest, and put it in a frying pan with the butter. Seal the meat rapidly. Season, drain and let it cool.

2. Using a coarse blade, chop the pheasant meat you set aside earlier with the chicken livers and pork in a food processor. Add the thyme, the diced pheasant, sugar, salt and pepper. Mix well and leave in the refrigerator overnight.

3. Prepare a glaze by mixing the egg yolks with a pinch of salt and a little water.

4. Roll out eight rounds of pastry 6 inches (15 cm) in diameter. Each should be about 1 inch (2.5 cm) thick. Keep them handy in the refrigerator.

5. Remix the forcemeat and divide it into four portions. Place a slice of foie gras in the middle of each portion, and mould each one into a ball.

6. Place four rounds of pastry on a baking sheet,

---

**SERVES 4**

**1 pheasant, boned**

**1 1/4 oz (30 g) butter**

**4 oz (100 g) chicken livers**

**4 oz (100 g) throat of pork**

**2 pinches of thyme**

**1 pinch (5 g) caster sugar**

**salt, pepper and flour**

**2 egg yolks**

**1 3/4 lb (800 g) puff pastry**

**4 slices of foie gras of duck,**

**weighing 1 1/4 oz (30 g) each**

---

glaze each one with a pastry brush and place a ball of pheasant and foie gras in the middle.

7. Cover them with the four remaining rounds of pastry, pressing along the rims to seal the pastry together well. Use a pastry cutter or a knife to trim them. Using a brush, glaze the tops and pinch the rim of each pie, then make some decorative markings on the surface with the point of a knife.

8. Place in the refrigerator for 30 minutes, then place the pies in a hot oven (425-450°F/220-230°C/Gas Mark 7–8) and cook for 20 minutes.

9. Serve immediately with a salad sprinkled with fresh walnuts.

*Serve with a rich,*
*smooth Puligny-Montrachet*
*Les Combettes 1983.*

Roast pheasant with endives, page 115.

# .HARE.

It is in autumn that the aroma of jug-ged hare permeates the kitchen. In ancient Greece, it was believed that eating hare beautified the face. Maybe that was the reason why Roman empe-ror Alexander Severus feasted on hare every day.

The male hare is called a buck, while the female is a doe. In France the hare is called a *financier* until it is four months old, at which point it weighs about 3 lb (1.5kg). At nine months, weighing approximately 5 lb (2.5kg), it is called a *trois-quarts*; at one year it is called *capucin*, and weighs 9–13 lb (4–6kg). For roasting and stewing, the most sought after is the *trois-quarts* which has arrived at the brink of maturity and weighs 4–6 lb (2–3kg). Any larger, and the hare's flesh becomes stringy and tough and should be used for pâtés, terrines, galantines or mousses.

You may recognize a young hare by the softness of its paws: its claws will be well hidden under its fur, its ears will taper to a point, its coat will be glossy. Avoid buying older hares, which may be detected by their long teeth, white fur near the muzzle and easily visible claws.

The best hares come from the plains of Brie, Beauce, Champagne, Gascony, Normandy and Poitou. Those from the mountains are excellent too, thanks to the tangy taste imparted by the local flora. You will also find on sale hares that have been imported from Eastern countries and South America. Some of them will have stringy flesh and poor flavour, and it is therefore regrettable that no legislation has been passed that requires hares to be label-led with their country of origin. If you have the choice, avoid the hare that has been shot in the chest as it will have lost much of the blood which is so vital for good fla-vour. Opt instead for one that has been shot in the head or shoulder, and insist on freshness, which may be judged by the brightness of the animal's eyes.

Hanging is not good for hare; it must be con-

*One senator's recipe for hare* à la royale *was the inspiration for the founding of a parliamentary group.*

sumed as fresh as possible. If you cannot eat it right away, it is best to leave it unskinned until just before you prepare it. Meanwhile, if a hunter offers you a hare that has not been killed cleanly or is damaged, you must skin and clean it as soon as possible. Wash its innards under cold running water, dry it with a cloth and daub it with olive oil. You should not marinate hare, unless you wish to preserve it, because its fine fla-vour will be altered by any sort of marinade. If you plan to sauté or jug it, you will get the best flavour by choos-ing the paws, thighs and shoulders. The saddle, or back of the hare, may be roasted, as in the recipe below. The liver, heart and lungs may be mixed with a little cognac or vinegar to keep moist.

It would be impossible to discuss this sprinter without mentioning *lièvre à la royale*, an admirable recipe which originated from an ancient quarrel between Poitou and Périgord. My favourite is that of the senator of Vienne, Aristide Couteaux, who at the end of the 19th century created a marvellous preparation of *lièvre à la royale* at the home of his friend Spuller, in Paris. Drawn by the exqui-site aroma of the dish, passers-by in the Opéra Comique quarter gathered under Spuller's window. The sensational recipe was published by the newspaper *Le Temps*, and ear-ned Senator Couteaux an invitation to the Palais du Luxembourg to expound on the details of this fine prepa-ration. A parliamentary group was founded, made up of the 'senatorial forks'. All this for a hare! The recipe became known as *lièvre à la royale, façon Aristide Couteaux*. For a long time, few restaurateurs offered this dish on their menu, perhaps because it was too traditional or old-fashioned. Now it is a dish that is back in vogue.

To me, it is a recipe that is fairly sparse. The hare is simply cooked in a red wine with garlic and shallots and thickened with the animal's blood. It is simply a matter of making a basic, slow-cooked compote of hare, seasoned with salt, pepper, thyme and enveloped in thin slices of bacon. In a large casserole, place 1 carrot cut into rounds, 2 onions studded with cloves, 20 cloves of garlic, 40 shallots and a bouquet garni, then the hare. Bring 2 bottles of Cornas wine to a boil, flambé it and pour it over the hare along with a large glass of good red wine vinegar. Cover the casserole and put it in the oven. After about 6 hours, the hare is cooked. Remove the hare and strain out the cloves of garlic and shallots. Strain the cooking juices into a pan and skim off the fat. Finely chop 5 shallots, 3 cloves of garlic and the liver, heart and lungs of the hare. Pour this mixture into the cooking juices, and put the pan over a low heat. Let it simmer for an hour and strain. Before serving, add the hare's blood to the sauce, along with a little bit of cognac. Put the pan back over a low heat and stir from time to time, without letting it boil, until the sauce is very smooth. Combine the bacon and the bones of the hare in the sauce with the cloves of garlic and the shallots. Heat well and serve with fresh pasta. Why the absence of foie gras? The highly seasoned flesh of the hare hardly needs it. However, I am not against adding a little foie gras to the sauce to soften it. If you wish to cook hare in *Périgordine* style, a whole foie gras is called for: it enriches and adds depth to the dish. Whether you consider it rustic or aristocratic, I would say the elegance and subtlety lies in the hare, and nowhere else.

Hare *à la royale*.

# SADDLE OF HARE WITH SHALLOTS AND MUSHROOMS

SERVES 2

**1 saddle of hare**

**3 oz (75g) butter**

**salt and pepper**

**thyme**

**2 shallots**

**7 oz (200g) mushrooms**

**2 fl oz (50ml) white wine**

**7 oz (200 g) crème fraîche**

**a hint of mustard**

**juice of 1/2 lemon**

1. Skin the saddle by inserting a knife blade under the skin and, little by little, sliding the knife between the skin and the flesh until it is completely detached.

2. Heat 1 oz (25g) of butter in a sauté pan. Once it is hot, brown the saddle on all sides then season with salt, pepper and thyme. Put it in a very hot oven (450-475°F/230-240°C/Gas Mark 8–9) for approximately 10 to 15 minutes, turning it midway through cooking. The meat should stay rosy. Take the meat out of the oven, remove it from the pan and season again.

3. In the same pan, heat 1 oz (25g) of butter and fry the shallots, which have been chopped beforehand into slices about 1/4 inch (6 mm) thick. Cook them for 5 minutes over a low heat. Add salt and continue to cook.

4. Remove the stalks of the mushrooms. In a frying pan, heat 1 oz (25g) of butter and sauté them briskly, then season with salt and pepper.

5. Combine the cooked shallots and the mushrooms. Discard the cooking juices, deglaze the pan with the white wine, and add the *crème fraîche*. Reduce, then add the mustard and the lemon juice. Pass through a sieve.

6. Place the meat on a serving dish, pour the sauce over it, add the shallots and arrange the mushrooms around the whole.

*Serve with a fine,*
*delicate wine from*
*the Côte-Rôtie.*

# .PORK.

*With a good*

*piece of pork*

*you can prepare real*

*gourmet fare.*

Since the dawn of humanity, pork has constituted an abundant source of nourishment for mankind. Many nations engage in the farming of this mammal, a member of the Suidae family. Authors of all nationalities allude to pork in their texts, and it is mentioned in the Bible.

Pork is often shunned for reasons of health. The Egyptians thought that pigs transmitted leprosy. Some religions proscribe the eating of pork on the grounds that its flesh is considered impure. Pork certainly does not keep well, and if it has begun to spoil it can cause illness such as botulism.

Today, there is no longer anything to fear. The handling of pork is closely supervised by the health authorities, in particular during the period between slaughtering and reaching the consumer – which does not always go hand-in-hand with its gustative quality. In fact, many pigs are fed scraps or cereal flours which have absolutely no beneficent effect on their flavour. However, from time to time pigs are allowed to wander free, grazing on natural foods and aromatic herbs which give their flesh a lovely, delicate aroma and a smoother quality. Under these circumstances, pork is among the most flavourful meat you will ever taste. Pork has the great advantage of being economical and it deserves more attention because it lends itself so well to a wide variety of recipes.

All parts of the pig are edible, from its head to its corkscrew tail. There are noble parts like the head – including the brain and tongue – which has numerous adherents; I serve it in my restaurant. A good piece of pork is recognizable by its fine texture, barely rosy tint, and white, firm fat, without a trace of moisture. Factory-farmed pork is both moist and whitened, and it is therefore bland. A dark, flaccid meat that is enveloped in a lot of soft fat is a sign of a mediocre animal.

Before refrigerators existed, most cuts of pork were salted in order to preserve them as long as possible. This custom endures because it gives certain cuts a very specific flavour. In the olden days, two degrees of salting were established: salted and half-salted. Today, the degree may vary – ask your butcher how much time you should allow it to soak before cooking. This might be from several hours to more than a day. Do not forget to change the soaking water several times. To soak pork well, the water should only be changed when it has become very salty. Water can only hold so much salt: the salt in the meat will no longer dissolve if the water has become like a pickling brine. On the other hand, if you change the soaking water of lightly salted pork the taste could be washed out, which is not desirable either. Also, certain cuts of smoked pork, such as the belly or the shoulder, should not be soaked.

Salt pork is most often boiled. Place the pork in a large quantity of cold water, unsalted of course. Most importantly, do not use warm water, or the flavour of the meat will be lost immediately. Add an aromatic garnish and let it cook in simmering water. Alternatively, certain cuts of salt pork may be braised with vegetables, cabbage in particular or, if the pork has been smoked, with sauerkraut.

Pork may also be enjoyed cold. Roast it as you would beef. To do so, buy cuts with the bone, the fat and, if possible, the rind: it will have more taste. Don't forget to add sage and garlic to the joint, since pork cannot do without them, and on occasion a little thyme and rosemary.

Fresh pork should be served well done: juicy but white, without a trace of pink. Served hot, it is delicious, but pork is perhaps even better cold, as long as it cools in the open air under a protective sheet of aluminium foil rather than in the refrigerator. As for its juices, there is no doubt that they are perfect for gracing a green salad. Fresh pork such as fillet may also be fried or grilled.

Pork forms the basis of stews from all regions. It may also be jugged: it is then thickened with blood as is the procedure for traditional, classic stew. Exotic prepara-tions with bitter-sweet sauces make pork a marvel, whe-ther the base is honey or pineapple – without forgetting a splash of vinegar, which brings it an indispensable aci-dic note. Contrary to received wisdom, good pork can make real gourmet cuisine.

# HONEY-ROASTED PORK

1. Prepare the pork the night before. Insert slivers of garlic all over the joint.

2. Roll the sage leaves between your palms, and then season them with salt and pepper. With the point of a small knife, make small slits between the ribs and insert the sage leaves.

3. Rub the roast with salt and thyme. Wrap it in clingfilm and place it in the refrigerator. The salt will have the effect of ageing the meat and bringing out the flavours of the herbs and garlic.

4. The next day, take the roast out of the refrigerator, wipe it and let it come back to room temperature.

5. Heat the oil in a casserole over a medium heat. When it is hot, place the loin of pork and the broken bones in the casserole. Let the meat brown, turning it from time to time. Add the onions and the bouquet garni. Cook for 3 or 4 minutes.

6. Cover the casserole and put it in the oven, which

**SERVES 6**

**3 lb (1.5kg) loin of pork, with broken bones**

**3 cloves garlic, cut into slivers**

**12 sage leaves**

**salt and pepper**

**2 sprigs thyme**

**2 medium-sized onions**

**1 bouquet garni**

**1 large carrot, sliced crosswise**

**2 tablespoons groundnut oil**

**2 spoonfuls red wine vinegar**

**2 tablespoons honey**

has been preheated to 400°F/200°C/ Gas Mark 6. Let it roast for 1 1/2 hours, tur-ning it often. Take the meat out and sea-son with pepper. Deglaze the pot with 1/2 pint (300ml) of water and let it boil lightly for 12 to 15 minutes until it has reduced by half.

7. Place the roast on the oven door. Turn the thermostat up to 475°F/240°C/Gas Mark 9. Dissolve the honey with the vinegar and baste the roast. Put it back in the oven for 12 to 16 minutes, basting it often. Let the meat sit for 15 to 30 minutes before carving.

8. To serve, carve the roast and arrange the slices on a warm serving dish. Pass the juice through a sieve and serve it in a gravy boat.

*Serve with a mellow white wine from the Loire, such as a young Coteau du Layon.*

# .WALNUTS.

Walnuts are harvested from their trees in autumn. Dubbed 'the royal nut' by the Greeks, walnuts were associated with bread, and were considered a food worthy of the gods of Olympus. The origins of the walnut tree, which go back to the dawn of time, are in the Middle East, where it grew wild. According to some historians, it originated in Persia.

*Walnuts and roast pork make a marvellous epicurean combination.*

Walnut trees have been cultivated in France ever since the Middle Ages, and were important for their wood and oil as well as their nuts. The latter have a green fleshy husk called a shuck that is rich in tannin. Green at first, the walnut turns brown as it ripens. The shuck draws back, and the nut itself appears in its hard shell. Inside the shell is a savoury fruit consisting of two hemispheres, which resemble those of the brain. This is no doubt the reason why the ancients believed that walnuts would cure a headache.

Harvest begins in October, as soon as the walnuts begin to fall. If left on the ground, they will rapidly deteriorate. If they are still imprisoned in their green envelope, other walnuts are piled over them and, a few days later, the shuck detaches. This also avoids tannin-stained hands.

Tasting a fresh, milky white walnut in the shade of the tree is a delight – but sleeping under that tree could be dangerous! Not so long ago, it was said that the cold, wet shadow could induce death. A good nut should have a dry shell, both inside and out. A very clean, bleached shell is not always a sign of quality: it often signals that the walnut has been treated and stripped with chemical products of questionable benefit. The flesh of the walnut should be healthy. The nuts are sold dry year round; if they are good quality they will feel heavy in your hand. Avoid any nut that is overdried, badly preserved, or has a mouldy odour.

Treatment of the flesh of the nut after shelling is becoming more and more mechanized. Shelling, however, is an operation that remains traditional and manual, done by encircling the shell with the point of a knife to extract the nut. The mixing and cold-pressing of walnut husks and flesh yields a delicious oil, with an intense flavour. Walnut oil should not be used in frying, since its flavour is too dominant. It will also quickly become rancid in light and will oxydize when exposed to air. Choose opaque rather than clear glass bottles, and always remember to replace the top right away. Its use for seasonings is a matter of taste – it is wonderful on salads composed of lamb's lettuce, endives, haricot beans and so on. Adding a dash of walnut oil to dried beans, as is customary in Poitou, transforms them into a real delight.

Walnuts have many uses in the kitchen, but do not store them in the refrigerator. Doing so makes their oil congeal and they become insipid. If soaked in milk, dried walnut flesh recovers its fresh flavour.

Nuts are classic in salads – who doesn't enjoy the combination? They are the ideal condiment for sauces and stuffings, and they go well with mushrooms, ceps in particular, and fish. They are equally successful with meats, especially pork, as in the following recipe: while you are roasting the pork, finely chop 40 shelled walnuts. Then, in a food processor, process 7 oz (200g) of sliced bread. Gently melt 4 oz (100g) of butter in a frying pan and add the breadcrumbs. Cook over a low heat, stirring constantly: the mix should remain frothy. If it is not, add a little more butter. Take the pan off the heat when the mixture is barely golden – be careful, since it will cook quickly. Put it all in a sieve and let it drain. Mix the breadcrumbs with the chopped nuts and season with salt and pepper. Stir and set aside. As soon as the roast pork is done, cover it well with this mix, then place it back in the oven until it is uniformly golden: there you have a real gourmet combination.

Gourmets appreciate walnuts with most cheeses, Roquefort being a remarkably good complement.

Walnuts are used primarily in confections and pastries as decoration or as an ingredient, either chopped or ground. They also make for delicious cakes.

T. 4 . N° 47

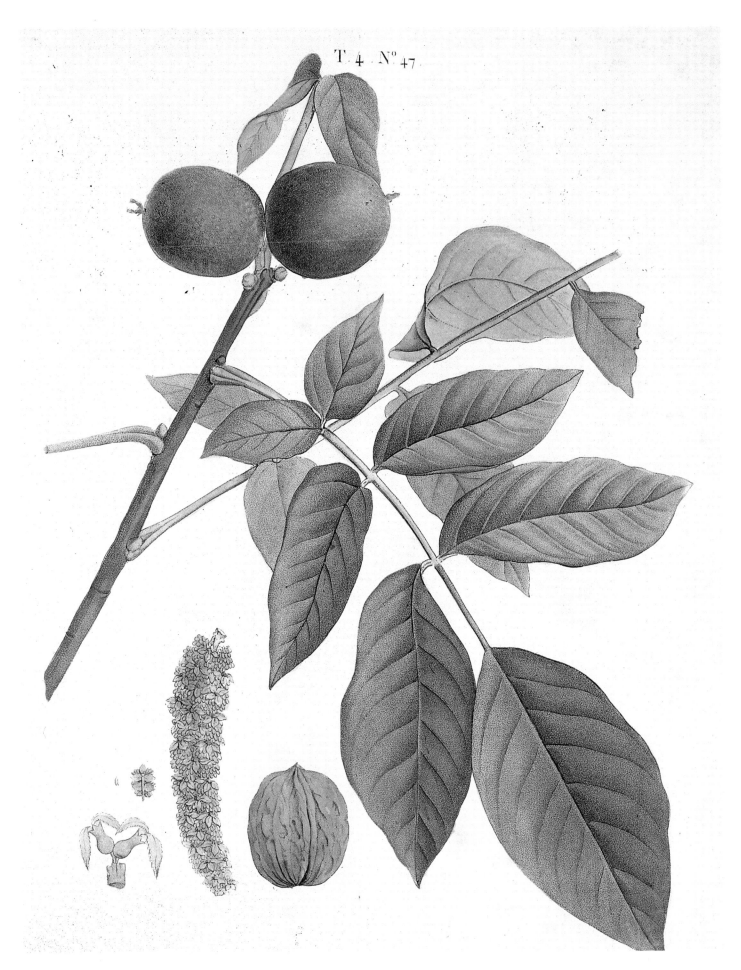

# CHOCOLATE CAKE
# WITH FRESH WALNUTS

SERVES 10

**9 oz (250g) softened butter**

**11 oz (300g) caster sugar**

**3 eggs**

**3 1/2 fl oz (100ml) warm milk**

**11 oz (300g) sifted flour**

**6 oz (175g) fresh walnuts, shelled, peeled and chopped**

FOR THE CHOCOLATE ICING

**4 oz (100g) of plain confectioner's chocolate**

**3 1/2 fl oz (100ml) cream**

**15 coarsely ground coffee beans**

**2 oz (50g) icing sugar**

1. With a whisk, mix the butter with the caster sugar. Add the eggs and warm milk and whisk well to obtain a mixture that is smooth and consistent.

2. With a wooden spatula, incorporate the flour and chopped nuts into the mixture. Pour the cake mixture into a buttered cake tin and bake for 25 minutes at 400°F/200°C/Gas Mark 6. When it is done, leave the cake to cool.

3. Melt the chocolate.

4. Bring the cream to a boil with the 15 coffee beans, then let it steep for 15 minutes off the heat. Strain the cream sauce and mix it with the melted chocolate. Set it aside in a cool place.

5. Cut the cake into three layers of equal thickness. Garnish the two bottom layers with the chocolate sauce. Cover the top layer with chocolate and sprinkle with icing sugar.

*Serve with a well-aged,
sweet Xérès.*

# .PEARS.

The juicy, fragrant pear is a delight. This member of the Rosaceae family traces its origins back to the Middle East, and is found growing wild in temperate climates in the Middle East and around the Caspian Sea. The fruit of such trees is small and sparse. The Romans would later remedy these drawbacks: as Virgil said: 'Graft your pear trees, Daphnis, your great nephews will reap the fruit.' Cultivation of the pear tree in France is a long tradition and there are a large number of varieties.

*The pear can be used in all kinds of recipes and is the fruit that best quenches thirst.*

The pear gave birth to many popular expressions such as *La poire est mûre* (the pear is ripe), meaning the moment is favourable; *Couper la poire en deux* (cut the pear in two), to share by half; *une bonne poire* (a good pear) is someone who is easily manipulated or duped. In olden days, it was customary to serve pears before the cheese course. To broach a subject *entre la poire et le fromage* (literally between the pear and the cheese) signifies waiting until the appetite has been sated and the diner is open to discussion. Pears make a tasty combination with cheese; try them with Roquefort and Cantal for a real treat.

Of all the fruit, the pear is the one which quenches thirst the best. There is a proverb that advises 'keep a pear for thirst', which highlights this property. Eating pears regularly guarantees a clear and healthy complexion and shiny hair. The pear is also full of vitamins, and is both a laxative and diuretic.

Pears come in different shapes: elongated or rounded, spherical or tapered. The colour of the skin is often green, turning to yellow in maturity. Certain types are stippled all over with russet or red spots. Pears may be bought year round, but autumn is their high season. The best time to pick them is when the fruit is ripe enough to break easily from its branch. Dessert pears, which are eaten raw, are often harvested before they reach maturity, since it is at the greengrocer's that they ripen completely. The time they will spend maturing here is so long that pears cultivated in autumn will not reach the market for comsumption until January or February.

A good, ripe pear will feel heavy in your hand and tender to the touch near the stem. It should be without spots or bruises and it should have either a lightly spicy or floral scent. A bruised pear becomes overripe quickly. Once ripe, pears will not keep for long.

The pear is put to many uses in a wide range of sweets and desserts. A classic of bourgeoise cuisine is compote of pears, which I prefer to make with red wine. Here's how: for 6–8 pears, boil 1 pt (600 ml) of red wine with 14 fl oz (400 ml) of blackcurrant syrup and a pinch of cinnamon. Meanwhile, peel the pears, cut them in half, remove the pips and rub the fruit with a cut lemon to prevent darkening. Then add the pears one by one to the wine and cassis, cover and cook, checking their progress. Once they are done, leave them to cool. They should be served with their syrup, thickened with a little cornflour that has been thinned with a teaspoon of boiling water. This pear compote is equally delicious with cinnamon ice cream or a pear sorbet.

Another classic preparation is *poire Belle Hélène* – pear poached in vanilla syrup and served with vanilla ice cream and chocolate sauce. This Parisian gourmet dessert owes its name to Offenbach's La Belle Hélène, which was composed in 1864. Don't forget pears in savoury preparations — they may be sautéed in butter as a garnish for duck, pork or game. Pears also go wonderfully well with spinach, not to mention spices such as pepper, ginger, cinnamon and mace. The pear may also be fermented into an alcohol, like cider: pear is unforgettable in an *eau-de-vie* which has been aged in a stoneware jug or in a bottle. The delicate aroma the pear develops as an *eau-de-vie* is very near that of the real thing. The pear is truly a versatile fruit.

# CARAMELIZED PEAR CAKE

SERVES 8

**12 oz (350 g) butter**

**9 oz (250 g) sifted flour**

**2 lb (1 kg) ripe pears**

**2 oz (50g) honey**

**9 oz (250 g) icing sugar**

**4 eggs**

**1/2 sachet of yeast**

**pinch of salt**

**2 oz (50ml) pear eau-de-vie**

**(optional)**

1. Butter and flour a cake tin and put it in the refrigerator.

2. Peel the pears and dice into 3/4 inch (2 cm) pieces. In a frying pan, brown them over a high heat with 3 1/4 oz (80 g) of butter. Add the honey and let it caramelize until it is golden.

3. With a whisk, mix 9 oz (250 g) of softened butter with the icing sugar. Incorporate the eggs one by one, then add the yeast, the rest of the flour and a pinch of salt. Gently add the caramelized pears and their juices.

4. Pour the mixture into the cake tin and bake at 400-425°F/200-220°C/Gas Mark 6-7 for 50 minutes.

5. Remove the cake from the oven, let it cool for 10 minutes, then remove it from the tin and put it on a wire rack.

*Slice the cake*
*and serve it with a chilled Muscat*
*de St Jean de Minervois.*

# .CHOCOLATE.

The magically rich and bewitching flavour of chocolate inspires pleasure and fascination. The Indians considered it a beverage of the gods. Chocolate is derived from the beans of the cacao tree, and may be classified as the crus are for wine, according to potency, flavour and varying bouquets. The selection and geographic origins of the cacao bean – Brazil, Ecuador, the Ivory Coast and Madagascar – are its determining factors. Chocolate, like wine, also has *appellations d'origine controllées*.

Once they have been chosen and tested, cacao beans are aired, brushed, and sifted to remove all debris. Next, they are roasted to allow their aromas to bloom and the shell to loosen progressively, which facilitates the final stage of grinding. The beans are reduced to large pieces by a vibrating sifter.

Then a very complex process for the chocolatier takes place: the selection and mixing of beans of different origins to make a good blend. The beans are placed in centrifugal mills which separate the fatty matter, the basis of cocoa and chocolate. Chocolate is obtained by mixing this basic ingredient with sugar, adding (or not adding) cocoa butter and aromatics, vanilla, milk and other ingredients. The chocolate is then subjected to a double grinding so that a homogeneous mixture may be obtained before the chocolate is kneaded for several hours. This operation, known as 'conching', aerates the chocolate, eliminates all traces of moisture and develops its aromas. As a result the chocolate becomes smooth, velvety and shiny. When brought to a precise temperature, it is ground and moulded into its definitive form.

A new trend has been developing among connoisseurs of chocolate: a preference for chocolate's characteristic sharp flavour, which is dominated by bitterness. The sugar and milk so loved by the Swiss and Belgians are being rejected, supposedly because they mask the flavour of the cacao bean. It is a stamp of authenticity, one which is required by the discriminating members of the *Croqueurs de chocolat* club, which was founded by the much-missed Jean-Paul Aron along with Claude Lebey and Nicolas de Rabaudy, both eminent gastro-

*The ideal accompaniment to coffee is a chocolate truffle.*

nomes. Chocolate which is free of all additives, should be of a pure brownish-red (rather than black) colour, smooth, shiny, and compact. It should boast a perfect homogeneity, a fine, uniform grain, and its break should be clean and dry. It should melt slowly on the tongue, without leaving a bitter or spicy aftertaste. Likewise, its aroma should not be even the slightest bit burnt or acidic.

To preserve chocolate well, you should keep it away from heat and humidity. Store it in a dry and airy place, at a temperature of 59-68°F (15–20°C). Chocolate is also very sensitive to other odours. Always leave it wrapped in its silvered paper and, if possible, in a tightly sealed container. The surface of a block of chocolate should be shiny and smooth. If it has been badly preserved or exposed to humidity, the chocolate loses its colour and lustre and tastes bland.

It would take too long to enumerate all the uses of chocolate. However, many recipes call for melted chocolate so it is worth discussing the best way to make that; melt the chocolate gently in a bain-marie at about 130°F (55°C) maximum, rather than in a saucepan directly over the heat, since its components risk separating over a too-high heat. One is often advised not to add any liquid to chocolate as it melts, for fear that it will solidify immediately, but what could be better than a little bit of coffee to reinforce the aroma of cocoa? Just take care that the coffee is the same temperature as the chocolate. Freeze-dried coffee lends itself well to this use, but in no way can adding coffee improve the chocolate if it does not contain enough cocoa. Take care to check the ingredients listed on the packaging: a good chocolate should contain no less than 55 per cent cocoa.

Chocolate truffles are the ideal accompaniment for coffee. To make them, grate 11 1/2 oz (330g) of bitter chocolate into a bowl and set aside another 7 oz (200g). Place 2 egg yolks in a separate bowl, add 2 oz (50g) of icing sugar and whisk until the mixture is pale and frothy. In a saucepan, combine 4 oz (100 g) of *crème fraîche*, 2 oz (50g) of butter and 2 oz (50g) of icing sugar. Allow the ingredients to boil just until they melt, and whisk them. Pour this sauce onto the egg yolks, whisking all the while, and then pour the liquid over the grated chocolate. Stir constantly. The chocolate will melt, but as a precaution, it is better to place the bowl in a large saucepan of hot water. When the chocolate has melted, add 2 fl oz (50 ml) of calvados and continue to whisk until the mixture is shiny and smooth. Place the chocolate in the refrigerator for a maximum of 1 hour. Then, using a pastry bag with a piping nozzle, squeeze 1/3 oz (10 g) dollops onto a sheet of grease-proof paper spread on top of a baking sheet. Place the truffles in the refrigerator for a few hours. They must be hard in order to be rolled. Melt the remaining chocolate then, using a fork, dip each truffle briefly in the chocolate. Roll them into a ball in the palms of your hands. Finish by rolling them in cocoa powder. Keep them in the refrigerator.

For parties I recommend this dessert, which I also serve in my restaurant.

# Chocolate Tart

Serves 8

**3/4 oz (20 g) butter**

**11 oz (300 g) sweet shortcrust
pastry**

**7 oz (200 g) confectioner's
chocolate**

**5 fl oz (150 ml) single cream**

**2 fl oz (50 ml) milk**

**1 egg**

1. Butter a flan ring with a removable base of approximately 8 inches (20 cm) in diameter.

2. Roll out the pastry until it is less than 1/16 inch (2 mm) thick and wrap it around the rolling pin to lift it to the flan ring. Unroll it, pressing it firmly so that it will adhere to the bottom and sides of the ring. Cut off the excess pastry around the sides and let the pastry shell sit in the refrigerator for about 30 minutes.

3. Preheat the oven to 400°F/200°C/Gas Mark 6 and cook the pastry shell for about 10 minutes.

4. During this time, cut the chocolate into small pieces and boil the cream and milk together in a saucepan.

5. Add the chopped chocolate, take the pan off the heat and whisk until the mixture forms a shiny, consistent batter. Then add the beaten egg and mix together well.

6. Pour the mixture into the precooked pastry shell.

7. Bake for 15 to 18 minutes in an oven preheated to 300°F/150°C/Gas Mark 2. The filling should be set, but not hard.

8. To serve, remove the sides and, if possible, the bottom of the flan ring. Serve warm or cold.

*'Hors d'Age' Banyuls
by Docteur A. Parcé
is the ideal wine to accompany
chocolate desserts.*

WINTER

# .SOUP.

Is the image of soup simmering in the corner of the hearth old-fashioned, or does it hark back to the basics of life? Soups, both hearty and refined, are coming back to our tables in force, and justly so. However, their history is richly varied, with as many detractors as admirers. Doctors at first advocated them, only to proscribe them later. Soups came into fashion and then in turn were forgotten. They have nourished children, peasants and workers, and appeared on the tables of kings, emperors and heads of state.

How I love the aroma of soup pervading the kitchen! For me, soup on the table evokes many images: the family reunited, childhood rediscovered; it is the course that one always had to finish in order to grow big and strong. In the past, the soup that simmered over the fire in a large pot – from which we get the terms *potage*, *potée* and even *potion* – constituted the family's main course, evolving into the more middle-class *potage*, which was served as an appetizer before dinner. Then came the more subtle consommé, which prepared aristocratic palates for the meal to come. Today, certain soups have re-emerged to gain favoured places on the menus of the world's top restaurants. For several years now I have served a savoury cream of broad bean soup, which has met with unexpected and resounding success.

Popular, hearty soup is often garnished with more solid nourishment: fresh or dried vegetables, chunks of meat, bacon, fish or shellfish or thick slices of bread. Onion soup from Lyon, Flemish stew, fish soup from the south of France, *chaudrée charantaise* (fish stew from Charentes), *garbure* (Gascon vegetable soup) from Les Landes and so on. One of the best, in my opinion, is *la petite marmite Henri IV*, a soup that combines vegetables, oxtail and giblets, and is served piping hot, enriched with croûtons and grated cheeses. What makes a soup good? It is like an infusion or an herbal tea. If it is too strong, it tastes pungent and bitter; not enough steeping makes it bland and insipid. Soup must be cooked just so, neither too much nor too little. Often, soup sits on the stove for too long, which gives it a disagreeable, strong flavour. To achieve the right flavour, it

*How I love the aroma of soup pervading the kitchen! Soup has regained its deserved place on the menu.*

is best to steam fresh vegetables (except for potatoes) first, then place them in a clear glass pan together with fresh butter and salt, and heat gently, to bring out all the flavours. But you must pay very close attention, for soups will become bitter if the vegetables are allowed to discolour or, worse, to burn. Let us move on to the details.

We shall begin, then, with the classic leek and potato soup. The method is very simple. Thinly slice 7 oz (200g) of leeks, and let them sweat for 3 or 4 minutes in a saucepan with 2 1/4 oz (60g) of butter and a pinch of salt, stirring constantly with a wooden spatula to avoid browning. Next, add 2 pt (1.2 litre) of water and a pinch of coarse salt. Add 1 1/2 lb (600g) of washed, peeled and quartered potatoes; cover, and leave to boil for 35 minutes over low heat. Next, run the mixture through the food processor, then return it to the heat and bring it back to a boil, adding 2 generous tablespoons of *crème fraîche*. Continue to heat for a few moments, adding 2 oz (50g) fresh butter, then purée in the blender and serve. According to the season, other vegetables may be substituted, such as carrots, turnips, garden peas and so on.

The same base may be used to create soups using dried vegetables such as lentils, split peas or haricot beans. But remember never to soak lentils or split peas; contrary to popular belief, they ferment and take on a bitter flavour. It will suffice to blanch them after washing. Bring them to a boil then refresh them, drain them and place them back in the saucepan. You can also vary the original recipe and prepare more rustic soups by dicing the vegetables rather than puréeing them.

The recipe offered here is a cream of pumpkin soup. The secret to preparing it lies in the final emulsifying which, when done correctly, gives the soup its velvety smoothness. The soup should have the consistency of custard. If you prefer vegetables other than pumpkin, you may also use this recipe as a guideline for preparing cream of cauliflower, asparagus or broad bean soup, all of which make excellent entrées to a wonderful meal.

# CREAM OF PUMPKIN SOUP

**1 3/4 pt (1 litre) chicken stock**

**2 lb (1 kg) pumpkin flesh, diced**

**1 teaspoon sugar**

**3/4 oz (20 g) cornflour**

**1/2 pint (300 ml) crème fraîche**

**4 oz (100g) butter, cut into small pieces**

1. In a saucepan, combine the chicken stock, diced pumpkin flesh and sugar. Bring the mixture to a boil, cover, and cook for 18 minutes. The pumpkin should be cooked quickly to avoid bitterness.

2. After cooking, blend in a food processor and then strain.

3. Return the mixture to the pan and bring it to a second boil. While stirring, be sure to scrape the bottom of the pan, as pumpkin burns easily. Skim off any scum that forms.

4. Blend the cornflour with 2 fl oz (50 ml) of cold water. Take the soup off the heat and add the cornflour, whisking it in well. Put the pan back on the heat and bring to a boil; add the cream and allow the soup to boil again. Mix in the butter. The result should be a smooth, creamy soup.

5. Place the soup back on the heat and taste. Do not add salt while cooking, since the seasoning from the chicken stock will usually suffice. Serve with sliced bread that has been fried in clarified butter.

# .CAVIAR.

Caviar, that food of luxury, is more than just a gourmet's dream. It is coveted for end-of-year festivities. Moreover, this most simple and magic of dishes was once a staple food for the impoverished fishermen of the Caspian Sea, which is the only place caviar worthy of the name is to be found.

Sturgeons are captured with extreme care at the beginning of spring and autumn. The fish is then knocked on the head. A Caesarian is performed immediately to liberate large sacs of roe which represent 10–12 per cent of the sturgeon's total weight. The roes are washed in pure iced water, then laid out and salted before being packed in their famous blue tins. All of these operations take place under the watchful eye of the 'master' who is as skilled as a master winemaker.

Whether it comes from the former Soviet Republic or Iran, caviar is given the same classification as the three types of sturgeon. Beluga is the most expensive. Its roes are the biggest, and may range from a light grey to a deeper colour.

Ossetra has smaller roe, which are of a greyish shade with russet tones. It is a little less expensive. Sevruga has even smaller eggs of a dark grey, almost black colour. It is the most common caviar and the least costly. Which should you choose? In the opinion of connoisseurs, Beluga would be the best. I prefer Ossetra for its hint of iodine. However, it is simply a matter of taste. The famous white caviar is that of the albino sturgeon. Its absence of colour made it a rarity which was reserved for the Shah of Iran, who gave it to his intimates, who in turn sold it to credulous dupes for astonishing sums.

Caviar needs no additions. Purists like it plain, without lemon juice, and most of all without that

*Among the wide choice of caviar, I prefer Ossetra for its hint of iodine.*

grotesque accompaniment of onions and hard-boiled eggs. Serve it with lightly grilled, well-buttered toast – alone, in majesty. To enjoy it at its best, take a little spoonful of caviar and keep it in your mouth, crushing the roe against your palate with your tongue rather than chewing. This is how caviar is savoured to perfection. Do not recoil at the thought of pressed caviar. Even though the presentation is less seductive, these burst roe are the vestiges of high luxury. For gourmets, pressed caviar is a concentrate of the best aromas of caviar, obtained from any of the three varieties. It requires 8 lb (4 kg) of roe to produce 2 lb (1 kg) of pressed caviar, and it sells for half the price. Enjoy it on warm blinis with *crème fraîche*.

In my restaurant, I serve caviar covered with a delicate, quivering aspic and a velvety cream of cauliflower. It is a dish that has become quite famous, but it is a fairly complex recipe.

One marvellous combination is that of smoked salmon and caviar. Purée 4 oz (100 g) of smoked salmon with 1 1/2 oz (40 g) of softened butter, three drops of *sauce anglaise* and 2 drops of tabasco sauce. With a wooden spatula, delicately incorporate 1/4 pt (150 ml) of whipped *crème fleurette* to the mixture. Place in the refrigerator for a minimum of 1 or 2 hours. To serve, use a small spoon to make quenelles of salmon and then top each with 2 teaspoons of caviar. Serve these 'frivolities of smoked salmon with caviar' with lightly toasted bread.

I suggest serving a well-chilled white Russian vodka with caviar. For celebrations, it's best to open a bottle of brut champagne, since it is the accessory to all crowning moments – if possible, serve a prestigious vintage.

Frivolities of smoked salmon with caviar, recipe p.142

# SLICED SCALLOPS WITH CAVIAR

recipe p.142

SERVES 4

**3 1/4 oz (80g) butter**

**16 large, very fresh scallops**

**4 oz (100g) caviar**

**1 teaspoon chopped lemon zest**

**juice of 2 lemons**

**approx 8 fl oz (250 ml) cream**

**Guérande salt and pepper**

**1/4 bundle of chives,**

**finely chopped**

1. Butter the bottom of four dishes. Finely slice each scallop into five rounds. Place 10 scallop rounds on each dish and put 1/4 teaspoon of caviar on top of each. Cover each garnished scallop with another round. With a brush, coat the scallops with softened butter.

2. Blanch the lemon zest in boiling water with the juice of 1 lemon. Refresh and drain.

3. Over the heat, reduce the cream until it is thick and velvety and add the juice of the second lemon. Season with salt and pepper. Incorporate 2 oz (50 g) of butter.

4. When you are ready to serve, gently incorporate the remaining caviar with the sauce. Put the four dishes in the oven for 2 minutes – just long enough to heat them without allowing them to brown.

5. Cover the scallops with the warm sauce. On each, sprinkle a little Guérande salt, the finely chopped lemon zest and a sprinkling of chopped chives.

*Serve*

*with a light, balanced*

*Chevalier-Montrachet.*

143

# .SALT COD.

Salt cod is a popular fish that is now very in vogue, which can only please the gourmet. It belongs to the genus of Gadus. A universal food, it has been the subject of diplomatic battles waged by seafaring countries. For a long time it was very inexpensive, but now its price rises constantly.

For centuries, cod nourished millions by virtue of its high preservability. The consumption of cod has increased greatly in inverse proportion to its availability. Known officially as the common codfish, polar codfish, fresh or frozen cod as well as salted cod, all may be found on the market. Today, as in the past, cod is caught using multiple tow lines. Once aboard, the fish is gutted, the head is removed and the liver, cheeks and tongue are set aside. One very ancient tradition is to dry cod. In olden days, fishermen prepared it themselves along the coasts of the New World, burying it under the sod and retrieving it during the following expedition. The winter climate froze it then thawed it progressively, which little by little had a dehydrating effect. Now, as soon as the fish is caught, it is salted while on board. In the past, during Lent, salt cod was served on every French table, whether aristocratic or the most modest. It is a fish that is full of cultural symbolism.

If you have already tasted a *brandade* of salt cod, you will know that it is one of March's treats. It eases the penitence of Lent because it is a splendid dish which has always been the delight of gastronomes. A good salt cod should have thick white fillets, with distinct, superimposed layers. Its colouring will be a bold brown on its back and silver on its belly. These signs show that a cod has recently been caught.

Salt cod should always be soaked in cold water before cooking. The duration of soaking varies with the thickness of the fish. In general, allow 24 hours for soaking cod if the fish is whole and 12 hours if it is already in fillets. Before doing so, take the time to wash the fish in a large basin and divide it into pieces of approximately 4 1/2 oz (130 g). Place it skin-side up in the bowl because if the skin is at the bottom, being impermeable, it will prevent the salt from settling at the

*Have you ever tasted brandade of salt cod? It is a March treat.*

bottom of the bowl. Place the cod in a sieve, then immerse the sieve in a bowl of cold water. The water should be changed at least twice. When it has soaked sufficiently, drain the fish.

Whatever recipe you choose, salt cod should be cooked either sautéed in oil or poached. In the latter case, put the pieces of fish in a large enough pan for there to be little overlapping. Cover them with lightly salted cold water. Add a bouquet garni. Place the pan over the heat. Watch carefully until the moment just before it starts to boil because even a little overcooking will cause the fish to harden and shrivel. The point at which the fish is about to boil is signalled by a thin white foam that rises to the surface and thickens, and it must be carefully removed at once or it will solidify and stick to the fish. At the first boil, take the saucepan off the heat, cover it and let it stand for 15 to 20 minutes. Alternatively, let it simmer over a low heat for 8 minutes.

Cooked this way, salt cod may be adapted to a wide variety of different culinary preparations, among them the succulent *brandade*, a recipe which is simple if you follow my instructions. Once the fish is poached, drain it, remove the skin if necessary, take out the bones and flake it into 2 lb (1 kg) of flesh. In a large casserole, heat 2 fl oz (50 ml) of olive oil. Add the fish and briskly sauté it, using a wooden spatula, until it is reduced to a fine paste. Put the casserole over a low heat and slowly incorporate 7 fl oz (200 ml) of olive oil, alternating with 3 1/2 fl oz (100 ml) of warmed cream. You will need half as much cream as oil, and it should be incorporated little by little, as if you were making a mayonnaise. Season with ground pepper and salt if necessary. Once done, the *brandade* is light, homogeneous and very white. For true luxury, add a few truffles.

There are innumerable recipes for salt cod. Once poached, it may be eaten warm in a salad with potatoes cut into rounds, onions, shallots and chopped parsley. The most famous recipe remains cod with Provençal *aïoli*. There are many variations of this typical spring dish, the only obligatory ingredients being

poached cod and steamed or boiled vegetables. Salt cod may also be savoured sautéed with olive oil with potatoes, onions and leeks, in sauce, in *croquettes* or in a *gratin*, and so on.

All the regions of the world that have access to the sea have left their culinary imprint on this fish. In Portugal, salt cod is called *bacalao* and is the national dish. Salt cod may be cooked in numerous ways – in fact, it is said that there are as many ways to prepare salt cod as there are days in the year!

# FRIED FRESH COD
## WITH CABBAGE

SERVES 4

**3 1/4 oz (80 g) smoked
salmon, thickly sliced**

**1 3/4 lb (800 g) cod fillets**

**1 large green cabbage**

**salt and pepper**

**olive oil**

**3 1/4 oz (80 g) butter**

**chervil**

1. Cut the smoked salmon into dice about 1/6 inch (4mm) thick. Cut the unskinned cod fillets into four slabs, or ask the fishmonger to do this for you.

2. Remove the leaves from the cabbage. Cut out the ribs and blanch the leaves in boiling salted water for about 10 minutes, then drain.

3. Season the cod fillets and fry them in a little olive oil in a non-stick pan for 5 minutes, skin-side up. Turn them over and cook for 3 minutes.

4. Cut the cabbage into strips of about 3/4 inch (2 cm), and put them with the butter in a saucepan over a low heat. Add the smoked salmon. Heat the ingredients and season them.

5. Arrange the cabbage on warm plates and place the fillets on top. Place a sprig of chervil on top of each piece of fish, as well as a pinch of Guérande salt and a turn of the pepper mill.

*Serve with a full,*
*fragrant, complex and delicious*
*white Château de Fieuzal 1986,*
*at a temperature of about 46–50°F (8–10°C).*

# .SALMON.

The salmon occupies a choice place at table. It would be a pity if its multiple origins – wild or farmed – erased from memory the taste of real, incomparable salmon of the Loire as I had the good fortune to enjoy it at the Tours restaurant of celebrated chef Charles Barrier.

From 15 November until the end of March the Loire salmon begin to swim upstream, unless the water level is too low. In this case they remain in estuary waters, where they wait for the rivers to rise again. These are winter salmon. The females are the first to migrate and they are very large, often weighing upwards of 26 lb (12 kg). They are followed by the males, which are smaller. The fish swim upstream toward the spawning beds along the banks of the Allier river. About three weeks later, the smaller spring salmon, which weigh about 9 lb (4 kg), arrive. By 15 May, the voyage has terminated. In mid-July, the gathering schools of fish are visible from the river banks, since the water level never exceeds 8–16 inches (20–40 cm). Worn out from their journey, the females lay their roe, which the males will later fertilize. The roe are guarded with extreme vigilance until the end of August or beginning of September. At the end of a few weeks (the exact period depending on the water temperature) the transparent fry hatch, then swim away with the current.

Salmon fry are the prey of other fish. Those that survive will continue downstream for six or seven months, at which time they are about as big as a finger. When they arrive in the estuary, they measure about 1 1/2–2 inches (4–5cm) in length and feed on plankton. From the estuary, they depart to complete their sea voyage. This mysterious journey is only partly understood – we are still unsure of the salmon's destination and the duration of the journey. Researchers have established that the fish go under the glacial ice caps, where shrimp and other nourishment abound, and it is here that the salmon flourish and take on their famous

*Rather than poaching salmon, it is preferable to grill it lightly.*

rosy colour. At the end of three years, the migration begins anew. The adults retrace their path, drawn by an almost magical instinct, and head towards their place of birth, where the life cycle is renewed.

Salmon is traditionally prepared poached, whole for the smaller fish and in steaks for the larger ones, and served with a mousseline sauce or a *beurre blanc* on the side. Served cold, poached salmon is accompanied by a mayonnaise or herb sauce. Salmon may also be braised in champagne or red wine. Nowadays, the tendency is to roast or cook salmon on the spit, either whole or in large steaks, or else to fry them in escalopes. Escalopes should be deboned and cut finely into fillets, each weighing 4 1/4–4 1/2 oz (120-130g). Flatten them carefully between two sheets of clingfilm, season them and then fry them rapidly in a non-stick pan with absolutely no fat. Salmon must be cooked very lightly, almost undercooked, so that it preserves its delicacy.

The great classic is the wonderful Troisgros recipe, *escalope de saumon à l'oseille*. It is served with a creamy shallot-based sauce with white wine and vermouth, seasoned at the last minute with sorrel, with stalks removed. Do not use lemon, and do not boil the fish. The marriage of fish and vegetables, though not new, came about because sorrel grows in February, just before the asparagus and garden peas which are traditionally served with salmon. Rather than poach salmon, I prefer to gently grill large pieces, glaze them with a little olive oil and then finish them in the oven. It is important to remember when cooking salmon that it must be just barely done and never dry.

# Grilled Salmon with Red Butter Sauce

**Serves 4**

**2 chopped shallots**

**18 fl oz (500 ml) full-bodied red wine**

**groundnut oil, salt
and ground pepper**

**9 oz (250 g) chilled butter,
cut in small pieces**

**1 good salmon steak,
approx 2 lb (1 kg)**

1. Place the chopped shallots, the wine and a dash of salt and pepper in a saucepan.

2. Bring the ingredients to a boil and allow them to reduce until only 3 soup spoons of liquid remain. Take the casserole off the heat for a few moments.

3. Incorporate a little butter with a whisk. Replace the saucepan over a low heat. When the butter is melted, add a little more bit by bit. When only a quarter of the butter remains, add salt and pepper and incorporate the rest of the butter off the heat; the sauce should never boil. If necessary, strain the sauce to remove the shallots. Keep the sauce warm in a bain-marie.

4. Baste the salmon with the groundnut oil and season it with salt and pepper. Grill it gently under a preheated grill for about 5 minutes on each side. Place it on a baking sheet. Finish cooking it for about 18 minutes in an oven preheated to 425°F/220°C/Gas Mark 7, turning it midway through cooking.

5. Remove the skin and place the salmon on a warm serving dish. Slice it finely in front of your guests. Serve the sauce in a warm gravy boat.

*Recommended wine:
an elegant and full Volnay, served
at a temperature of 59–60°F (15–16°C).*

# .CAPON.

A truffled, golden brown, stuffed capon is the feathered queen of the Christmas season. It has been a party dish since antiquity, and the Romans are credited with the idea of castrating cock birds.

From the Middle Ages to the 17th century, the capon was the most highly prized fowl in France. With time, it was replaced by the fattened pullet and the turkey, which was brought over from America. Recently, the capon has come back into fashion and its fine, delicate flesh is the centrepiece that marks holiday feasts. It comes originally from the region of Le Mans (Loué) in southwestern France but now comes primarily comes from Bresse, where production is limited to the end of the year in order to preserve its quality. But why, one might ask, is the cock castrated? It is done in order to confer on a mass of masculine muscle the voluptuous and tender curves of the opposite sex. Castration makes the bird fat, and his flesh becomes tender. Breeders must pay careful attention to the food and living conditions of the bird, for a capon must be of top quality. Care is lavished upon it as if it were the aristocrat of the farmyard. Nothing is refused it, and it roams freely, enjoying a grassy terrain and varied diet for many months. Then, around the end of November or beginning of December, the bird is placed in a hen coop, where it is fattened. The exceptional flavour of the Bresse capon makes it the most wonderful fowl in the world – a gift from heaven and the farmer.

*Freedom to roam and a varied diet – the capon is refused nothing.*

First, you must learn to choose capons well. The skin should be satiny, without the little yellowish dry spots that are the signs of bruising. It should be fresh but not wet. Pass your finger under the wing, near the joint – if you find the skin a little wet or sticky it means that the bird is less than fresh.

For all large birds, turkey or capon, it is necessary to remove the tendons from the thighs, which would be too tough to eat. To do this, make an incision with the point of a knife along the length of the foot. Open and expose the cluster of five or six tendons. Slide a trussing needle under one or two of them, no more. Pull them out firmly, so as to detach those that are lodged deeper in the drumstick. It is best to arm yourself with a cloth. Once the bird has been cleaned, you may dress it with truffles, if you wish. Gently slide one or two fingers between the skin and the flesh up by the neck to separate them and continue on along the thigh toward the rump, without damaging or puncturing the skin. Finely slice the truffles, dip them one by one in oil and slide them carefully under the skin of the bird. Fold the skin of the bird's neck back along its back to close it, sew the bird up and season it.

Capon may be cooked in many ways. The best and most traditional way is on the spit over an open fire. Barding is unnecessary. Though often done by merchants, it can damage the bird. As for stuffings, those with a sausage or chestnut base ruin the taste of the bird and never cook as quickly as the bird does. Instead, try the following stuffing recipe. The ingredients are somewhat complex and therefore more taxing. But the quantities are small and, after all, not every day is a holiday!

If you roast the capon on a spit, you should use a brush to baste it with softened butter. If you are roasting the bird in an oven, place it in a roasting pan with three or four knobs of butter. Contrary to conventional practice, begin with a cool oven so that the bird will be more tender. Add the pinions and chopped trimmings, and half a head of unpeeled garlic. For a bird weighing over 9 lb (4 kg), proceed as you would for turkey:

poach the capon gently in chicken stock for 20 to 25 minutes without allowing it to boil, then roast it. Do not put it in the oven to roast on its back; rest it instead on one thigh so that the fat and juices penetrate the breast. Turn it so it rests on the other thigh, being careful not to pierce its flesh. Do not add water as it will soak the bird's skin. Baste it with fat only. In the oven, the bird should brown slowly, as the temperature is gradually turned up from 300°F/150°C/Gas Mark 2 to 425°F/220°C/Gas Mark 7. Allow 2 1/2 to 3 hours' cooking time for a bird of approximately 8–9lbs (3.5-

4kg). When it is almost done, place the bird on its back so that it will have an even colouring, then take it out of the oven. Season again with salt and pepper. Lightly skim off the excess fat and add a little cold water to the pan juices. Allow to boil, scraping the bottom of the pan well and strain the juice. Serve with a celery *purée,* chestnut *confit* or a lamb's lettuce salad with truffles. Pierre Perret, a fine chef, gentleman and gastronome, adds an endive *confit* to the gravy.

Serve this holiday dish with a strong, full Pomerol, served just slightly chilled.

# STUFFING FOR TRUFFLED CHRISTMAS CAPON

INGREDIENTS FOR 1 CAPON

**2 oz (50g) bacon, finely diced**

**4 oz (100g) chicken livers,**

**finely diced**

**salt and pepper**

**5 oz (150g) raw or cooked**

**foie gras,**

**finely diced**

**1/3 oz (10g) truffles, finely**

**chopped**

**(use more if you wish, there**

**can never be too many!)**

1. Fry the bacon.

2. Remove the pan from the heat and add the chicken livers.

3. Return the pan to the heat for a few moments, briskly sauté the livers, then season with salt and pepper.

4. Transfer the cooked livers to a bowl and place them in the refrigerator.

5. Once cool, add the *foie gras* and truffles, mixing them together well.

6. Stuff the capon with this rich preparation which will nourish and perfume the flesh of the bird by pervading it from the inside, especially in the case of those cooked on a spit.

# .POT-AU-FEU.

The *pot-au-feu* is one of the most popular dishes in France. Originally, it was the pot bubbling on the hearth that gave rise to this rustic, flavoursome recipe which warms the body when chilly weather sets in. To make a good *pot-au-feu*, everything depends on attention to detail and deliberate slowness.

First, ask your butcher for a very fresh piece of beef, as opposed to a simple cut you would buy to roast, grill or fry which may have been kept slightly longer. Select a piece of silverside if possible; for an even richer taste, you could add a rack of ribs and oxtail. An excellent *pot-au-feu* results in large part from the abundance of meats. The leftovers will contribute to delicious dishes such as beef salad, shepherd's pie and the *miroton* (boiled beef and onions) so dear to Simenon. In my opinion, the secret ingredient is ginger. Even those who claim not to like the latter love my *pot-au-feu*, to which I add finely julienned ginger just before serving. Ginger produces a freshness that enlivens *pot-au-feu* and aids digestion. Note, though, that it must be added at the end of the preparation, because if it is thrown in with the other ingredients, the flavour will dissipate. Also indispensable are carrots, leeks, celery and turnips, which may be replaced with the more savoury parsnip, though it is rare and difficult to find. I never use bay leaves, which tend to dominate and overpower the other flavours.

Since the ingredients are not thrown in the pot all at the same time, nor are taken out at the same time, the easiest thing to do is wrap them by category in clean muslin cloths or large squares of gauze, which are available at the chemist. That way, they are easy to remove once they are cooked. They must then be kept warm in a little stock and reheated just before serving. *Pot-au-feu* may be enjoyed with cabbage or potatoes. If you serve it with cabbage, blanch the leaves before cooking them separately in a little stock. Potatoes should likewise be cooked separately, rather than in the *pot-au-feu*, or else the dish will be merely a stew. As meats are added to the stock, any fat

*Discover the splendour of the convivial pot-au-feu.*

should be skimmed off the surface. To do this, pour a little ladleful of cold water into the pot so that the fat congeals on the surface and can be easily removed. When the cooking is finished there should be very little fat left. Skim it off with a ladle, along with a little stock, and set it aside to be used in the next step.

In the refrigerator, soak the marrow bones in salted water for 8 hours or so beforehand. Then drain them and place them in a saucepan, and pour the fatty stock over them. Let them simmer for about 10 minutes.

The secret of the clarity of the stock lies in a slow cooking, during which the meat blanches. The pot should simmer constantly but never boil. Some cooks say that the stock smiles! Before adding the meat to the pot, it must be boiled in water for 5 minutes, then rinsed in cold water. This does not mean you should dispense with skimming the stock at the first simmerings of the *pot-au-feu*.

I could not describe the splendour of *pot-au-feu* without recounting the one I served to a group of gastronomes, including the food critic Michel Piot of the *Figaro*, who described it as the stuff of legend. I started by serving a *foie gras*, poached in stock along with with some vegetables from the pot, sliced and seasoned with *fleur de sel* and a pinch of coarsely ground pepper. Then the classic rack of ribs, an essential, was followed by a truffled *poularde* from Bresse, also poached in the *pot-au-feu* stock. Then another white meat, a delicate knuckle of veal, lightly cooked. The surprise course was lamb poached in stock, of course, as were all the other meats – tender, without the slightest tint of pink, and of an inimitable flavour. This was followed by finely sliced duck, bolstered by a marrowbone, half-salted belly of pork, pearly rose in colour with translucent fat, the saddle slow-cooked until it melted in the mouth, sweetbreads prepared with pistachios, and *sabodet*, the speciality of the great *charcutier* Bobosse of Bordeaux. Then, to finish, a deboned oxtail was accompanied by a fresh marrowbone, as if to punctuate the meal.

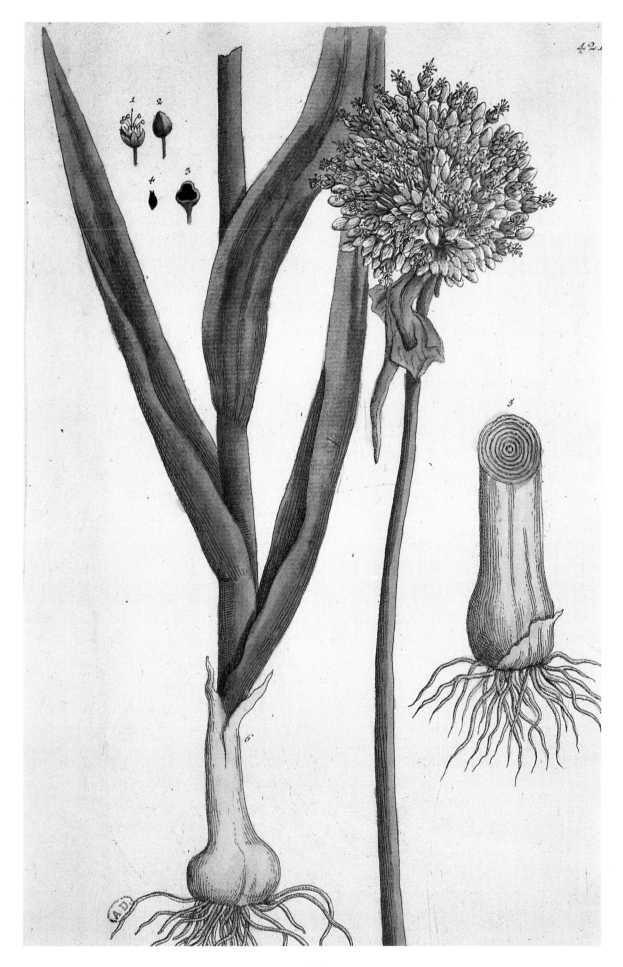

# FIVE-MEAT POT-AU-FEU

SERVES 12

**3 lb (1.5 kg) shin of beef**

**2 1/2 lb (1.2 kg) knuckle of veal**

**2 1/2 lb (1.2 kg) leg of lamb, trimmed**

**1 poularde and 1 plump duck, cleaned and trussed**

**12 small marrow bones**

VEGETABLES, PEELED AND WASHED

**24 small carrots**

**24 small leeks**

**12 small parsnips or turnips**

**12 sticks celery, sliced into thin batons**

AROMATICS

**3 medium onions**

**6 cloves**

**5 cloves garlic**

**15 black peppercorns**

**1 large bouquet garni, made of leek greens, celery, thyme and sprigs of parsley**

**2 oz (50g) coarse salt**

**2 oz (50g) fresh ginger, minced**

1. Blanch all the meats for 5 minutes and rinse in cold water.

2. In a 5 1/4 gal (24 litre) casserole, place the shin of beef and cover it with 2 gal (9 litres) of cold water. Bring it to a simmer.

3. Halve the onions horizontally and place them in a non-stick frying pan, flat side down, over a medium heat. Brown them for 4 to 5 minutes until they are quite golden and caramelized, so that they will add flavour and colour to the stock. Stud them with cloves.

4. Halve the cloves of garlic lengthwise and remove the sprouts. Tie them in muslin with the peppercorns.

5. When the water in the casserole is simmering, add the onions, bouquet garni and the bundle of garlic and pepper. Season with salt and partially cover the casserole to limit evaporation. Continue to simmer.

6. After 2 hours' cooking, add the carrots and celery. Fifteen minutes later, add the leeks, tied in a bundle, and the parsnips. Cook for 45 minutes, then remove the vegetables and set them aside in a saucepan of stock.

7. Add the knuckle of veal and lamb. Cook for 45 minutes. Then add the poularde, duck and ginger. Continue to simmer for about 45 minutes and check to be sure that all the meats are done. Set the casserole aside, off the heat, for 30 minutes.

8. During this time, skim off the fat and a little stock, pour it over the marrowbones, which have been soaked beforehand, then put in a saucepan. Bring to simmering point and gently poach the marrowbones for a few minutes.

9. When you are ready to serve, reheat the meats, vegetables and marrowbones and arrange them on plates. Let your guests cut the meats and serve themselves, for the *pot-au-feu* should be a party dish. Season with Guérande *fleur de sel*, ground pepper, gherkins, pickled onions, mustard and perhaps grated horseradish.

*As an accompaniment
I recommend serving a young and fruity
Savigny-lès-Beaune or a St Emilion
such as the Château Cadet-Bon, which
I serve in my restaurant.*

# .LENTILS.

January is a month for gourmets, for family dinners and for dinners among friends. The art of eating well is poetry for the body. We need warmth and good food. This is the ideal time to appreciate lentils, which were immortalized in the Old Testament: Esau sold his birthright for a plate of them.

For a long time, lentils were the food of the impoverished and humble, the caviar of the poor. Today lentils have earned the approval of nobility and gentry alike, and they may be found in numerous dishes, often traditional, regional specialities. Moreover, it is recommended that children eat lentils for their nutritive value. The best are the small green variety from Puy, which are more tender than the larger yellow variety grown in the north of France. Fresh lentils are extremely rare.

Before cooking, lentils must be washed with care because they may be dusty. Soaking them the night before is a serious error. Though received wisdom says that this makes them more tender and digestible, in fact the contrary is true: they begin to germinate and ferment, which is bad for both their flavour and your health. Most important, never use the soaking water to cook the lentils. It is best to blanch them by plunging them into cold water, bringing them to a boil, and draining them straight away. This eliminates bitterness and any traces of preservative. You may add a spoonful of bicarbonate of soda, which reacts with the calcium in the water to facilitate cooking and make these dried pulses more tender. The best way to cook lentils is with spring water – a rustic dream!

Once the lentils have been blanched and drained, put them back in the saucepan with plenty of water because they will swell. Always use cold water, as you do when blanching. You will need at least three parts water to one part lentils. Use no more than a teaspoon (5g) of salt per 1 3/4 pt (1 litre) because it will concentrate as the water evaporates. Cook over a low heat without covering the pot. Skim the surface of the water. Once it becomes clear, after 10 to 15 minutes, add an aromatic garnish – a bouquet garni, onions studded with cloves, carrots, smoked belly of pork and garlic. If the water has

*The little green lentil has earned a noble place at the table.*

evaporated add more, but make sure it is hot. The lentils should be well covered. Cover the casserole and allow 45 to 60 minutes' cooking time according to the variety of lentil.

Lentils go very well with pork, duck, game and anything that is fatty, such as *foie gras*. They are served hot or cold in a salad, a *purée* or in soup.

Bacon is a simple and delicious accompaniment for lentils. You will need a fatty cut, finely diced. In a frying pan, heat the bacon until the fat runs and add chopped onions. Let them sweat gently, then add smoked belly of pork, cut into small lardons, and let it sweat some more. Add a little finely chopped garlic, the cooked lentils and some of the cooking juices. When you are ready to serve, add a knob of butter.

# KNUCKLE OF PORK WITH LENTILS

SERVES 4

**4 half-salted knuckles of pork**

**9 oz (250g) Puy lentils**

**3 medium onions, 2 carrots, 3 cloves garlic**

**salt and pepper**

**4 oz (100g) smoked belly of pork**

**1 1/2 oz (40g) fatty bacon**

**2 3/4 oz (80g) butter**

**3/4 oz (20g) chopped parsley**

**2 bouquets garnis, 2 cloves**

1. Soak the knuckles of pork for approximately 8 hours. Drain and grill until the skin comes away from the bone. Cook for about 2 1/2 hours in water with an onion studded with cloves, a bouquet garni, a carrot and whole peppercorns.

2. Blanch the lentils and drain them. Put them back in a saucepan and begin cooking in cold water with a 1/2 onion studded with a single clove, 1 carrot, 2 cloves of garlic and a bouquet garni. Add salt.

3. Finely dice the smoked pork and the bacon. Once the lentils are cooked, remove the aromatic garnish.

4. Heat the bacon in a frying pan until the fat runs. Add 1 finely chopped onion and a dash of salt and cook it without letting it brown. Add the smoked pork and heat the mixture well. Add the cooked and drained lentils, along with a little juice left over from cooking the knuckles.

5. Continue cooking for a few minutes and add a little chopped garlic and parsley. Correct the seasoning if necessary.

6. Pour the lentils onto plates and place the pork on top. Serve hot.

*Recommended wines: from the Rhône Valley, a Crozes Hermitage or a Côte-Rôtie that is not too young; from Bordeaux, select an elegant and structured Pomerol.*

# .CABBAGE.

This vegetable, which boasts a long culinary history, displays its green maturity in autumn. When the weather is ruthlessly cold, it makes a comforting vegetable from the kitchen garden. Greeks and Romans ate cabbage at large banquets to stave off the effects of too much alcohol. Pythagoras recommended it and Diogenes, that barrel-bound cynic, ate only cabbage and water. He attained the respectable age of 90 – quite a feat in those days. Is cabbage a secret ingredient to a long life? Cato, who expounded upon its merits, certainly thought so.

Cabbage often figures in everyday expressions: in French, *une feuille de chou* (a cabbage leaf) is a downmarket newspaper, a rag. *Etre dans le chou* (to be in the cabbage) means to faint or to be nearing the end, *aller planter ses choux* (to go and plant cabbages) means to retire to the country.

Cabbage originally grew wild on the northern coastlines. It was a sea kale, the ancestor of all cabbage varieties, a hardy plant with large, thick, smooth, wavy-edged, lightly waxy leaves. Appreciated first for its medicinal qualities, the cabbage rapidly became a precious source of nourishment and constitutes the base of many stews.

There are two large groups of cabbage that are grown in cultivation, the round type with very tightly held leaves which may be white, green or red, and kale, which has curly green or violet leaves. Everyone has his or her favourite!

Buy a fresh cabbage that has been recently cut. It should be heavy for its size. The leaves should be shiny and firm, they should squeak under your fingers and give off a drop of water when they are broken. The cut of the stalk should be clean, without discoloration.

*Stuffed cabbage is a rustic, hearty dish, a staple of family-style cuisine.*

Cabbage does not keep well, so it must be cooked without delay. Remember that a cabbage shrinks by more than half while cooking.

To prepare cabbage, begin by removing and discarding the large outer leaves. Cut out the stem and quarter the cabbage. Remove the central core without separating the leaves too much. Wash them in a large basin of vinegared water, spreading them out well to remove any earth or insects. Then place the quarters in boiling salted water, cooking them in turn if you do not have a large enough pot. Boil on a high heat for 10 to 15 minutes until the cabbage is fairly tender. Cool the quarters in iced water, then drain quickly. Press them firmly between two flat plates to remove excess water.

Cabbage may then be prepared in many ways, including this recipe: cut the blanched cabbage into strips about 3/4 inch (2 cm) wide. Put them in a saucepan over a low heat with a knob of butter. Heat and add seasonings. Serve this as a garnish for fish, poultry, ham, game, and so on. A young spring cabbage does not need to be blanched; it may simply be sliced and cooked in butter.

Stuffed cabbage is a welcoming regional recipe which warms the body when the thermometer drops. It is a rustic, family-style dish which, over time, has lost none of its seduction, even if the old quarrel over the stuffing endures: should it be placed in the heart of the vegetable or between the leaves before reconstructing the vegetable? It is an unending debate!

In certain regions, such as in my native Poitou, stuffed cabbage is garnished mainly with vegetables including lettuce, leeks, parsley, spinach, sorrel, beets, heart of cabbage, garlic, onion, slices of bread, eggs and a little belly of pork. Cabbage is the best complement for pork.

Cabbage also makes a good trimming for other vegetable garnishes which are rare in winter; it lends itself to many appetising possibilities, both classic and modern.

## Braised Green Cabbage

SERVES 4

3 tablespoons goose
fat or butter

2 medium onions

2 peeled minced carrots

nutmeg, salt and pepper

1 blanched green cabbage

5 juniper berries

11 oz (300g) half-salted
belly of pork

1 bouquet garni

18 fl oz (500 ml) chicken
stock or water

1. Place the goose fat, onions and carrots in a large casserole that will fit in the oven. Season with a dash of salt and let them sweat for 5 minutes without browning.

2. Unwrap the leaves of blanched cabbage and remove the large midribs. Add the cabbage to the pot with salt, pepper, a little ground nutmeg and the juniper berries. Mix the ingredients well.

3. Bury the pork and bouquet garni in the cabbage.

4. Pour the chicken stock into the casserole and bring it to the boil. Cover with greaseproof paper (cut to the size of the casserole) and then the lid. Put in the oven and let cook for 1 1/2 hours at 425°F/220°C/Gas Mark 7.

5. When it is done, remove the bouquet garni and the pork. Slice the pork and add it to the cabbage.

6. Serve the braised cabbage with pork or game, especially partridge or roast pheasant.

*Serve with*
*a red Hermitage that has aged*
*for a few years.*

# .POTATOES.

The potato is the most popular vegetable in France. I don't know anyone who can resist a plate of crisp fried potatoes or a smooth potato *purée*.

According to Doctor Patrick P. Sabatier, the potato is a nutritional food: when eaten fresh, it compensates for deficiencies in the modern diet, which is generally low in complex carbohydrates and limited in mineral salts. Contrary to received wisdom, potatoes are not fattening. From February to July, new or spring potatoes appear on the market. When you go shopping, remember that the skin of the potato should be smooth and taut, and the flesh should be firm. Bruises, sprouts or eyes are defects and diminish the potato's gustatory qualities.

Choose potatoes that are medium-sized, and of a regular form and uniform size. The large ones have little flavour, and are only worth while for making chips. If you decide to cook them in their jackets, wash them in a basin filled with water, brushing them if necessary to remove all traces of earth. When they are peeled, diced, cut into rounds, into chips and so on, potatoes release a whitish juice that is partly composed of starch. This must be eliminated or the potatoes may stick together while cooking, take on a reddish colour and fail to become crisp. To wash them well, plunge them in water and drain (do not put them in a sieve, or the starch will wash off one potato onto the others).

The most traditional way of cooking potatoes is with water, which brings out their flavour. If you prefer to cook them peeled, do not cut them into small pieces or they will become saturated with water and disintegrate. Choose a potato that holds together well, like Roseval or Rate, all of the same size so that the cooking will be uniform. Place them in a large saucepan and cover them with cold salted water. Never use hot water, which will make them mushy. Bring the pot to a boil but do not boil the potatoes too hard: a light simmering will suffice. The cooking time varies with the type and size of the potato, but allow about 25 minutes. Test by piercing the potato with a knife; if they are done the blade should come out clean, with no residue. If you cook new potatoes in salted water

*Here is how to succeed in making smooth and creamy mashed potatoes.*

they will disintegrate; it is better to salt them a few minutes before you finish cooking.

To make good mashed potatoes like the kind I serve in my restaurant every day, peel and then immediately place the potatoes in cold salted water and cook them. Use medium-sized potatoes, since the little ones make for dry mashed potatoes while the big ones are too watery. Avoid using new potatoes, which make for dense, elastic *purées* (if you are preparing new potatoes, cook them in their skins). Be very precise about the cooking time; they should be medium-done. If the potatoes are undercooked, the purée will be lumpy; if they are overcooked, it will disintegrate. Remove them from the pan with a slotted spoon and place them in a colander; their own heat will make the extra water evaporate. Mash them immediately, using an old-fashioned manual masher with a fine mesh, without attacking too many at once. Avoid electric mixers, which make sticky mashed potatoes. Then place them in a casserole. Now is the time to add fresh butter – not at the end! Place the casserole on the heat and incorporate the butter, knob by knob, with the aid of a wooden spatula, while heating gently. Taste and season if necessary. Add boiling milk to obtain the desired consistency, which varies according to taste. You may finish by whisking it to make it lighter. If you're looking for perfection, pass the mashed potato through a fine sieve, which will make it more smooth and creamy.

Potatoes lend themselves to many types of recipes, and are often prepared fried. How I love fried potatoes! After cutting and washing, I recommend plunging the potatoes for 1 or 2 minutes into a large pan of unsalted boiling water. Drain and allow to cool (thanks to this process the fried potatoes will be golden, crisp and delicious). Then plunge them for the first time in oil at 320°F (160°C) and let them cook for about 10 minutes. The potatoes should be cooked in the middle, yet remain white. Take them out, then plunge them a second time in hot oil at 350°F (180°C). A thermometer is almost indispensable to success. In olden days, potatoes were fried in deep black frying pans. I am in

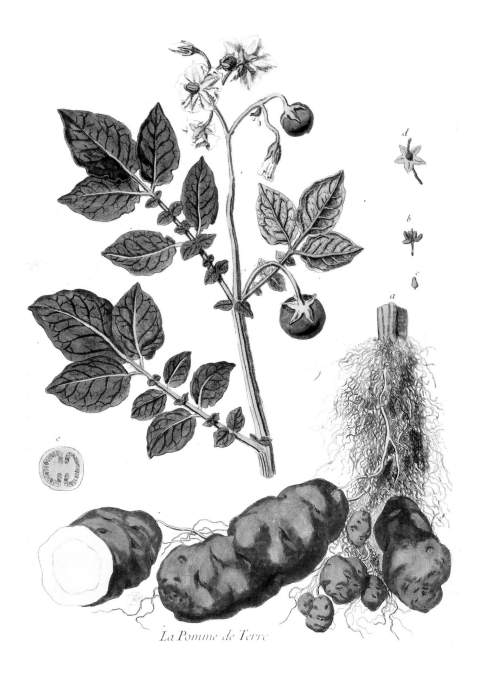

*La Pomme de Terre*

favour of this approach as long as you do not put in too many potatoes at once, and as long as they are cooked in two steps. Whatever the method, they should be drained on paper towels and sprinkled with salt. Personally, I always mix coarse and fine salt, for a seasoning that crackles a little between the teeth – a delight! It is a recipe which was passed on to me by my friend the excellent chef André Moreau, who is a native of Chablis, when I worked in the Berkeley on the Champs Elysées back in the 1960s. The restaurant turned out to be something of a breeding ground for future culinary stars among its alumni are Alain Senderens, Henri Faugeron, Guy Ducrest to name just a few. In Burgundy, the land of prestigious vintages, the harvesters prepare the following hearty dish before heading out into the vineyards. When they arrive in the fields in the morning, they build a bonfire using vine shoots. Then, as the harvesters toil away in the vineyards, a pot full of smoked pork-covered potatoes cooks on the hot embers.

# HARVESTERS' POTATOES

SERVES 6

**2 1/4 oz (60 g) butter**

**5 oz (150 g) smoked belly of pork, thinly sliced**

**2 1/2 lb (1.2 kg) potatoes, sliced in rounds 1/8 inch (3mm) thick**

**4 oz (100 g) grated Gruyère**

**5 oz (150 g) half-salted pork, thinly sliced**

**ground pepper**

1. With a brush, butter the inside of a cast iron or copper pan.

2. Cover the bottom and sides of the pan with smoked belly of pork, overlapping the sides of the pan.

3. Layer the potatoes, Gruyère and half-salted pork in the pan. Season with pepper. Do not add salt.

4. Cover the potatoes with the slices of smoked pork that overlap the pan.

5. Sprinkle the ingredients with knobs of the remaining butter. Cover with a sheet of aluminium foil and a lid. Place in an oven preheated to 425°F/220°C/Gas Mark 7. Cook for 1 1/2 hours. Then press down the ingredients with a slotted spoon.

6. Take the pan out of the oven and let it cool for 15 minutes.

7. Using a knife blade, loosen the smoked belly of pork from the sides of the pan and unmould the dish onto a plate. The ideal complement to this rustic and succulent potato cake is a leg of lamb or a side of beef.

*Serve with
a good red Bordeaux, Burgundy,
or Côtes-du-Rhône. Try a Médoc vintage
like Ducru-Beaucaillon '81, a Pommard Rugiens '83
or a Châteauneuf-du-Pape '86.*

# .TURNIPS.

*Nothing is more fragrant and delicate than new turnips.*

How lovely is the tender turnip! As soon as spring returns, it pokes its nose out of the ground. The turnip's origins are ancient – after all, it formed the base of our ancestors' diets, along with cabbage, until the discovery of the potato. It heralds from the Middle East, China and the Mediterranean basin.

Once scorned, the turnip has regained its place in the sun thanks to modern cuisine – which is a good thing, since it never really deserved to suffer the indignities it has endured over the centuries. In France, everything that is a failure, or insipid and colourless, is described as a *navet*, or turnip. If a painting is bad, we call it a 'turnip'. A play which drives spectators away is a *navet*. This is without a doubt the basis of the prejudice the turnip has suffered so long. We should lose no time in repairing such a sin. Nothing is better, more perfumed and delicate than tiny new turnips decorating a roast duck. Because they absorb fat, turnips also make a good garnish for *foie gras*, fatty meats, lamb, pork, boar, and so on. You will discover in cooked turnips a singular, succulent flavour.

The most important thing to know is how to choose a good turnip. The flat and round ones are often more tender than the longer variety, which are stringier. New turnips are generally sold tied in bunches. Choose fresh, firm ones by checking their leaves, which should be green and not wilted. The turnip's skin should be clear of spots and tender. All stringy or spongy turnips should be discarded.

To prepare turnips, peel them carefully, since they have two skins. For new turnips, trim the stems to about 2 1/4 inches (6 cm) and wrap them in aluminium foil for protection. If they are slightly older, cut a little cone around the base of the stem and remove it. To avoid darkening, peel and wash turnips just before cooking them. At the end of the season, they will require blanching to modify their strong flavour. This is not necessary for the tender, less bitter new turnips.

The most classic way to prepare turnips is to glaze them. It is a slightly complex but delicious recipe. Place the turnips in as large a saucepan as possible and fill it with water. Add fine salt, 2 1/4 oz (60 g) of butter and 2 teaspoons (10 g) of sugar for each 18 fl oz (500 ml) of water. Place over the top a piece of greaseproof paper which has been cut to size and buttered, butter side down. Thanks to this improvised lid, the water will evaporate little by little. The turnips are done when no water is left, and they will be slightly golden, barely coloured, and glazed with butter and sugar.

New turnips are delicious in a salad: peel them and plunge them in boiling salted water for 7 to 10 minutes, depending on their quality and freshness. Drain and cool. Slice them and toss them in vinaigrette. The young leaves may also be eaten in a salad and they are an excellent accompaniment to roast meat, chicken and rabbit. Turnips have long been used in soups and *pot-au-feu*. It is the principal garnish for *navarin*, that ragout of mutton whose name is probably derived from this vegetable (*navet*). But the best recipe for new turnips is to steam them in a gravy.

# NEW TURNIPS
# STEAMED IN GRAVY

SERVES 4

**2 lb (1 kg) little round turnips**

**1/2 oz (15 g) caster sugar**

**salt and flat parsley**

**3 1/4 oz (80 g) butter**

**3 1/2 fl oz (100 ml) chicken stock**

**3 1/2 fl oz (100 ml) chicken gravy**

1. Carefully peel the turnips, trying to keep them about the same size.

2. In a bowl, mix them with sugar and salt.

3. Finely chop the parsley.

4. Heat the butter in a large sauté pan. Once it foams, arrange the turnips side by side (they should not overlap). Brown them evenly.

5. When they are quite golden, sprinkle the turnips repeatedly with the chicken stock. Cover and steam them over a low heat.

6. Once cooked, arrange the turnips on a serving dish and pour the hot chicken gravy over them. Top each turnip with a little chopped parsley.

*Serve with a meat –*
*duck, for example –*
*accompanied by a spicy,*
*full red wine such*
*as a Madiran.*

# .CHESTNUTS.

The autumn chill coincides with the return of chestnuts, that food of Jack Frost, the shepherds of Ardèche and the mountaineers of Cévennes or even Corsica.

What distinguishes the humble *châtaigne* from the *marron*? It is a simple matter of whether they come packed together in the same husk or singly. You should buy chestnuts that have a beautiful, shiny, dark brown peel and flesh that is as fresh as that of a newly sliced potato. Avoid chestnuts that lack lustre and have distended skin.

To cook chestnuts as they are done by the vendors who park their carts at market, choose chestnuts that are flat on one side and well-rounded on the other. Success in cooking them rests on the split of the chestnut's skin – a badly split one will burst or cook poorly. Holding the chestnut in your left hand, use the point of a sharp knife to split the skin of the round side lengthwise without piercing the flesh. This is the most important point. If the split is not well done, the steam cannot escape fast enough and the chestnut will cook too quickly and crumble. While cooking, the chestnut loosens and swells due to the steam, and its skin grows brittle. If the chestnut is split at the pointed end, there will not be enough room for it to expand and it will compress. Next, place a frying pan over a low heat and add the chestnuts, spacing them well so that they do not touch. Cover and stir from time to time. At the beginning a lot of vapour escapes from the chestnuts. After 15 or 20 minutes, a slight smoking indicates that they are done. This is the time to remove the skin. To do so, turn up the heat. Then, after browning them well, turn them onto the flat side and lightly burn them. This way, the skin will come off on its own. Peel chestnuts by cutting the peel on the rounded side, then place them in

*In the holiday season, the chestnut attains a noble stature when paired with turkey, and is a triumph in desserts.*

the oven in a shallow pan with a thin layer of water for 7 or 8 minutes. Peel them while they are still hot. Another way of peeling them is to follow my method; I peel them by splitting them and putting them in small quantities in a very hot fryer for 2 or 3 minutes. Drain and peel immediately.

Chestnut purée is a classic garnish which is ideal for poultry, meat or game. To make a fine, savoury and light purée, put the peeled chestnuts in a saucepan and cover them with milk. Bring them to a boil, add a bouquet garni of a celery stick and a little sugar. Put the pan over a low heat and cover. Cook gently and consistently until the moment the chestnuts crush easily between your fingers. Allow about 1 hour to prepare them, since this should be a slow cooking. Once cooked, drain the chestnuts and put them through a food processor or a fine sieve in small quantities so that they will stay hot. Once they are puréed, place the chestnuts back in the pan, add knobs of butter and whisk. Then, to obtain a creamy purée, add warm *crème fraîche* a spoonful at a time. Heat the ingredients over a low heat, and do not let it boil as this will spoil the flavour of the butter.

Chestnuts may be used in many other recipes. Some regional ones include braised chestnuts, or cabbage and chestnuts, or they may be used in stuffing for poultry and so on.

These recipes show that the chestnut has come a long way from the time the poor dubbed it 'the bread tree'.

## CHESTNUT CONFIT
## WITH SMALL ONIONS AND WALNUTS

SERVES 4

**2 lb (1 kg) chestnuts**

**4 oz (100 g) small onions**

**8 shallots**

**1 very small bulb of fennel**

**4 oz (100 g) butter**

**1 1/4 pt (700 ml) chicken stock**

**3 1/4 oz (80 g) fresh**

**shelled walnuts**

**salt and pepper**

1. Peel the chestnuts, onions and shallots. Slice the fennel bulb lengthwise.

2. Heat the butter in a deep sauté pan. Add the onions, shallots, fennel and chestnuts and brown them lightly.

3. Add the chestnuts, arranging them alternately with the onions, shallots and fennel.

4. Add the chicken stock, bring it to the boil and cover the pan. Season to taste.

5. Let the ingredients cook for about 40 minutes, stirring as little as possible so as not to damage the chestnuts. Remove the lid.

6. Reduce the liquid, then roll the chestnuts, onions, shallots and fennel in it so that they are covered in a shiny coat.

7. Add the walnuts and continue to cook the mixture for another 5 minutes.

8. Serve the chestnut confit in its jus as a side dish for meat or poultry.

*Serve whatever wine you have chosen*
*to accompany either meat or poultry.*

# .LEMON.

The perfumed, juicy lemon is a concentrate of the sun's rays. Originally from India, the lemon tree grows wild in the regions south of the Himalayas. The Hebrews naturalized lemons in the valleys of Palestine. The Greeks and Romans imported it from Persia, and it inherited the name 'Medea's apple tree'. Later, in Pliny's time, it took the name *citrus*. Crusaders had the good idea to spread lemons throughout Europe, and cultivation developed in the Mediterranean basin.

*Concentrate of the sun, the lemon is the fruit of the tree which belonged to Medea.*

The lemon tree is a vigorous plant which can reach up to 16ft (5m) high. Its big green leaves are lanceolated, and were at one time used to make crowns to adorn the heads of the immortal gods. The lemon tree may flower many times a year, at which times it is covered with white petals tinged with purple, bunched in fragrant bouquets. You may easily find a lemon tree in many stages of development simultaneously, both in bloom and bearing clusters of fruit. Since it is sensitive to the cold, the lemon tree prefers gentle, slightly humid climates, and it bears fruit from May to October.

The pretty yellow lemon is generally oval-shaped. Its thin rind encloses many segments of fine, juicy and bitter pulp. The lemon is a concentrated form of vitamins, organic acids and enzymes. It has been featured throughout the centuries in medicinal and folk remedies, but these have largely been abandoned. The great navigators embarked with large quantities of lemons, for nourishment as well as to stave off scurvy and maladies caused by eating foods which have been conserved too long. The Arabs used the lemon as a remedy for snake bites and poisonous plants. It is a natural antidote for poisonous mushrooms, toxic mussels and bad water; it possesses astonishing properties for combating infection, anaemia and stress, among other maladies, and is used for stopping bleeding. It is truly Mother Nature's blessing.

The lemon also figures in everyday expressions. *Presser quelqu'un comme un citron* (squeeze someone like a lemon) means to draw the maximum out of them; *être jaune comme un citron* (to be yellow as a lemon) means to have a poor, sallow complexion; *se presser le citron* (to squeeze the lemon) means to rack the brain over something.

When shopping, you may recognize good lemons by their sweet fragrance, weight, clear yellow colour and ripeness. When well ripened (which you may distinguish by the fineness of the peel) lemons are more flavoursome and produce more juice. The greener the stem, the fresher the lemon. Look at the labels: wholesalers and greengrocers are obliged to note whether the fruit has been waxed or not. In any case, it is advisable to wash lemons carefully. If you are planning to use its peel it is better to purchase a lemon that has not been waxed, since the substances used to preserve it are toxic and insoluble. In addition to what everyone already knows about lemons, it is also used as an anti-oxidant to prevent the darkening of certain fruits and vegetables. In many seasonings, it replaces vinegar as a condiment and adds fragrance to sauces, seafood, fish, meats and vegetables.

The lemon is found in numerous sweet dishes, creams, mousses, entremets, jellies, preserves and sorbets. Its uses are considerable. Perhaps that is why it is the symbol of hard work!

cl. Pillenreuth

Königsweyher

# LEMON CHARLOTTE

SERVES 10

CHOCOLATE BISCUIT

**6 eggs**

**3 1/2 oz (90 g) plus 1 1/2 oz (40g) caster sugar**

**4 oz (100 g) and 1 oz (25g) flour**

**1 oz (25 g) cornflour**

**1 oz (25 g) cocoa powder**

**1 1/4 oz (30 g) icing sugar**

**1 1/4 oz (30 g) butter**

LEMON MOUSSE

**4 oz (100 g) crème fleurette**

**3 oz (75g) and 2 oz (50g) caster sugar**

**3 eggs**

**3 fl oz (75 ml) lemon juice**

**grated zest of 1 unwaxed lemon**

**2 sheets of gelatine**

**4 teaspoons Cointreau mixed with 4 teaspoons water**

1. Whisk 6 egg yolks with 3 1/2 oz (90 g) of caster sugar and set aside.

2. Mix 4 oz (100 g) flour with the cornflour and cocoa powder. Set aside.

3. Beat 6 egg whites with 1 1/2 oz (40 g) of caster sugar until stiff, then combine them with the yolk and sugar mixture. Then, using a wooden spatula, delicately incorporate the cornflour, flour and cocoa mixture.

4. Using a piping bag, make large nest-shaped biscuits on a baking sheet that has been buttered and floured. Powder them with icing sugar and bake them for 8 to 10 minutes in an oven preheated to 350°F/ 180°C/Gas Mark 4.

5. In a bain-marie, heat the *crème fleurette* with 3 oz (75g) of caster sugar and 3 beaten egg yolks. Let it set lightly. Add the lemon juice and grated zest. Whisk the mixture until it thickens, then remove it from the heat. Add the 2 sheets of gelatine, which have previously been softened in cold water. Let this lemon cream cool, but do not allow it to harden.

6. Beat the 3 remaining egg whites with 2 oz (50g) of caster sugar until stiff and gently incorporate this with the lemon cream sauce.

7. Line a charlotte mould with the biscuits which have been lightly soaked in Cointreau. Fill the interior with lemon mousse. Put it in the refrigerator for at least 2 hours, then unmould.

*Serve with*
*a well chilled wine,*
*such as a late-vintage*
*Gewurztraminer.*

# .FLAKY PASTRY.

Since the beginning of time, the holidays have been celebrated with various forms of traditional cakes. The first Sunday in January, the day of Epiphany, we 'crown' kings with a flaky cake, hollow or with filling, or with a *brioche* cake. In the past, a real bean was baked inside the cake, symbolizing the embryo, the sign of life to come.

Nowadays, an enamelled porcelain charm, often of a baby, is used. Later came other charms: a moon, a king, a clover leaf and even a *louis d'or* (an old gold 20-franc piece) which blessed the lucky person who found it on his or her plate. Who has not eyed the *gateau des rois* (king's cake) in search of a little swelling that would indicate the treasure's hiding place? Who does not hold his or her breath as the cake is cut? And what a strange privilege is granted by the bean! It bestows on whoever receives it the right to be king for a day. The king drinks and, in certain regions, chooses a queen, to whom he offers another cake.

This traditional king's cake starts with puff pastry. You can buy it ready-made, which will give good results. Making the pastry from scratch is agony for some amateurs. However, if you follow my instructions, this pastry should be (almost) easy to make well. And what a pleasure, what happiness – your light and golden galette will only be better for it.

A bit of vocabulary first: a *detrempe* is a paste of flour, water and salt. Often, a little butter is added to make it more supple and facilitate the process of successive folding. A puff pastry dough requires a very fine layering of butter and *detrempe*. In practice, the butter is encased between two layers of *detrempe*, which is then thinly rolled and then folded into three. This is called one turn. Since this step is repeated six times, at the end you should have many hundreds of layers. In the heat of the oven the butter melts, and the void it leaves is accentuated by the evaporation of the water in the *detrempe.*

There are a few precautions that you should take. Your work surface should be smooth and cool; the ideal

*Becoming a master of puff pastry is really quite easy.*

surface is a marble slab. You will also need a large rolling pin and a soft brush to get rid of excess flour. Use a very fine flour. Choose a high-quality butter, preferably one that contains as little water as possible. The secret to success is that the butter and the *detrempe* remain the same consistency. For this reason, the first thing to do is let the butter soften. The *detrempe* may be made by hand or in a mixer, but always avoid warming it. However you mix it, always allow the *detrempe* to sit for 20 to 30 minutes so that it will regain its elasticity. Before you begin rolling the pastry, here is a trick of the trade: each time you use the rolling pin, press it down a little at both the top and bottom of the dough. This permits it to be rolled easily without deforming the borders.

In addition, you should dust the table and the pastry with flour between rollings so that the pastry will not stick. Before folding it in three, brush off all the flour that remains stuck to the pastry. Try to keep a consistent pressure on the rolling pin as you roll so that the edges stay parallel. Never push too hard. Each time you spread out the pastry make sure the corners are at right angles or you will end up with different thicknesses. If small bubbles appear, it is important not to pierce them. They will reabsorb on their own.

Do not forget to spread out the pastry in the other direction after each turn, doing so by giving the pastry a quarter-turn. To know where you are, mark the pastry with your fingers every two turns: first two, then four, then six. After every two turns, let the pastry sit in the refrigerator for 20 to 30 minutes. The pastry is now ready.

Glaze only the centre of the pastry with a beaten egg yolk – never the sides, or the pastry will not rise properly.

To bake, moisten the baking sheet before placing the pastry on it to reduce shrinkage. It is important always to remember to let the pastry sit in the refrigerator for a minimum of 30 minutes before putting it in the oven to bake.

# KING'S CAKE WITH PINEAPPLE

SERVES 5 OR 6

**8 inch (20 cm) cake**
**1 1/4 lb (500 g) puff pastry**
**1 egg yolk for glazing**
**5 fine slices of fresh**
**pineapple, quartered**
**icing sugar**
**1 dried bean**

FOR THE ALMOND CREAM

**2 1/4 oz (60 g) ground**
**almonds**
**2 1/4 oz (60 g) icing sugar**
**2 1/4 oz (60 g) butter**
**1 whole egg**
**1 spoonful double cream**
**2 teaspoons dark rum**

1. Spread out the pastry in two rounds the size of a large plate and place them in the refrigerator to stiffen.

2. In a mixing bowl, combine all the almond cream ingredients and mix them for 3 minutes until they start to blanch.

3. Prepare the glaze by thinning the egg yolk with a few drops of water.

4. Place a round of pastry on a baking sheet. Cover it with the almond cream, leaving a 3/4–1 1/4 inch (2–3 cm) border all around. Slide the bean into the almond cream and decorate the top with the pineapples.

5. With a brush, moisten the border, cover the cake with the second round of pastry and press the sides together to seal the cake.

6. Using a brush, glaze the surface of the cake with the egg yolk.

7. Decorate the surface of the cake with the point of a knife, making sure the incisions are very superficial – no deeper than 1/16 inch (1mm). On the border, make little oblique incisions. Place the sheet back in the refrigerator for 30 minutes before cooking to avoid any loss of shape.

8. Bake for approximately 30 minutes in an oven preheated to 400°F/200°C/Gas Mark 6. As soon as the cake is done, remove it from the oven, then preheat the grill. Powder the surface of the cake with icing sugar and let it sit under the grill for a few seconds. The cake is best served warm.

*Serve with a richly aromatic,*
*intense Muscat*
*de Beaumes-de-Venise.*

# RECIPES

# INDEX

Lobster Fried *à la Meunière* 62
Lobster with Sauternes 64
Roast Lobster 62

**Melon**
Melon Sorbet with Banyuls Sauce 79

**Morel**
Braised Morels and Asparagus with Chervil 21

**Mullet**
Fillets of Mullet in Olive Oil 74

**Mushroom**
Saddle of Hare with Shallots and
Mushrooms 119

**Mussel**
Hot Mussels with Cold Tomatoes 69
Mussel *Éclade* 60
Mussel *Mouclade* 60
Mussels *à la Marinière* 60
Mussels with Chives 61

**Olive Oil**
Fillets of Mullet in Olive Oil 74

**Onion**
Broad Beans and Baby Onions with Smoked
Bacon 34
Chestnuts Confit with Small Onions and
Walnuts 169

**Oyster**
Hot Oysters 96
Poached Oysters 97
Warm Oysters with Fennel and Curry 98

**Partridge**
Roast Partridge 112
Suprême of Partridge with Cabbage and
Foie Gras 113

**Pastry**
Flaky Pastry 174
Short Crust Pastry 86

**Pear**
Caramelized Pear Cake 130
Compote of Pears with Red Wine 128

**Pheasant**
Pheasant and Foie Gras Pie 116

**Pineapple**
Kings' Cake with Pineapple 176

**Pork**
Honey Roasted Pork 121
Knuckle of Pork with Lentils 159
Roast Pork with Walnuts 124

**Pot-au-Feu**
Pot-au-Feu 154
Five Meat Pot-au-Feu 156

**Potato**
Fried Potatoes 162
Harvesters' Potatoes 164
Leak and Potato Soup 138
Mashed Potatoes 162

**Pumpkin**
Cream of Pumpkin Soup 140

**Purée**
Chestnut Purée 168
Mashed Potatoes 162

**Salmon**
Frivolities of Smoked Salmon with Caviar
142
Grilled Salmon with Red Butter Sauce
149

**Salt**
Roast Leg of Lamb with Herbs and Salt
Crust 26
Sea Bream in a Salt Crust 71

**Savory**
Savory Broad Bean Soup 32

**Scallops**
Braised Scallops 101
Fried Scallops 100
Grilled Scallops 100
Scallop Salad 100
Sliced Scallops with Caviar 143

**Sea Bream**
Sea Bream in a Salt Crust 71

**Shallots**
Saddle of Hare with Shallots and
Mushrooms 119

**Sorbet**
Grapes Sorbet with Sauce 81
Melon Sorbet with Banyuls Sauce 79
Strawberry Sorbet 44

**Soup**
Cream of Pumpkin Soup 140
Leek and Potato Soup 138
Savory Broad Bean Soup 32
Strawberry Soup 45

**Strawberry**
Strawberry Sorbet 44
Strawberry Soup with Orange Flower
Water 45
Wild Strawberry Short Crust Tart 88

**Stuffing**
Truffled Christmas Capon Stuffing 152
**Tart**
Apricot Tart 46
Apricot Upside-down Tart 47
Chocolate Tart 134
Wild Strawberry Short Crust Tart 88

**Tomato**
Cod with *Dugléré* Sauce 69
Hot Mussels with Cold Tomatoes 69

**Truffle**
Truffle and Smoked Bacon Pancakes 94
Truffled Christmas Capon Stuffing 152

**Tuna**
Tuna Omelette 67

**Turnip**
Glazed Turnips 166
New Turnip Salad 166
New Turnips Steamed in Gravy 169

**Vanilla**
Caramelized Custard with Brown Sugar 50
Vanilla flavoured *Crème Anglaise* 48

**Veal**
Rolled Veal and Kidneys 30

**Walnut**
Chestnuts Confit with Small Onions and
Walnuts 169
Chocolate Cake with Walnuts 126
Roast Pork with Walnuts 124

# ILLUSTRATIONS

pp. 8 & 118  Hare, *Œuvres Complètes de Buffon.* © Jourdes-Édimages – Bibliothèque de l'Institut, France.

p. 120  Pork, *Œuvres Complètes de Buffon.* © Jourdes-Édimages – Bibliothèque de l'Institut.

p. 125  Walnut, *Redouté* engraving, © Jourdes-Édimages.

p. 129  Pear, Revue Horticole. © Kharbine-Tapabor.

p. 133  Cocoa, *The Blackwell Herbarium,* Nuremberg, 1757. © Jean-Loup Charmet – Bibliothèque des Arts Décoratifs, France.


**WINTER**

p. 139  Pumpkin, *Album Vilmorin,* 1871. © Vilmorin-Andrieux.

p. 142  Sturgeon, 18th century engraving. © Jean-Loup Charmet.

p. 145  Cod, 18th century engraving. © Jean-Loup Charmet.

p. 148  Salmon. © Jourdes-Édimages.

pp 150-151  Capon. © Bibliothèque Nationale, France.

p. 155  Leek. © Jourdes-Édimages.

p. 158  Lentils, *Plantes de la France,* vol.7 by M. Jaume Saint-Hilaire, 1820. © Édimedia – Private Collection.

pp. 9 & 160  Cabbage, 16th century engraving. © Jean-Loup Charmet – Bibliothèque Nationale, France.

p. 163  Potato, *La Botanique mise à la portée de tout le monde par les sœurs Regnault,* Paris, 1774. © Jean-Loup Charmet – Bibliothèque Nationale, France.

p. 166  Turnip, German engraving, circa 1750. © Jean-Loup Charmet – Bibliothèque des Arts Décoratifs, France.

pp. 9 & 168  The Common Chestnut, botanical plate, end 19th century. © Jean-Loup Charmet – Bibliothèque des Arts Décoratifs, France.

p. 171  Lemon. © Ariel Press, 1990.

p. 175  Making Butter, 16th century German engraving. © Jean-Loup Charmet – Bibliothèque des Arts Décoratifs, France.